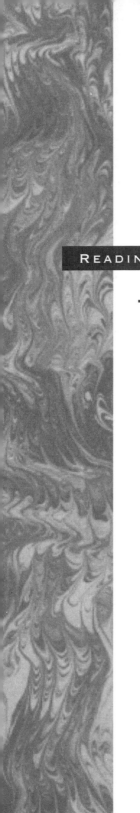

THE COMEDIES

THE GREENHAVEN PRESS
Literary Companion
TO BRITISH LITERATURE

THE COMEDIES

David Bender, *Publisher*
Bruno Leone, *Executive Editor*
Scott Barbour, *Managing Editor*
Bonnie Szumski, *Series Editor*
Clarice Swisher, *Book Editor*

Greenhaven Press, San Diego, CA

Library of Congress Cataloging-in-Publication Data

Readings on the comedies / Clarice Swisher, book editor.
        p.   cm. — (Greenhaven Press literary companion
to British literature)
    Includes bibliographical references (p.) and index.
    ISBN 1-56510-574-5 (lib. : alk. paper). —
ISBN 1-56510-573-7 (pbk. : alk. paper)
    1. Shakespeare, William, 1564–1616– Comedies.
2. Comedy. I. Swisher, Clarice, 1933–   . II. Series.
PR2981.R43   1997
822.3'3–dc20   96-19957
                                                              CIP

Cover photo: © Corbis-Bettmann

Copyright ©1997 by Greenhaven Press, Inc.
PO Box 289009
San Diego, CA 92198-9009
Printed in the U.S.A.

> **"All the world's a stage,
> And all the men and
> women merely players."**
>
> *As You Like It*, act 2, scene 7

CONTENTS

Chapter One: The Spirit and Development of Shakespeare's Comedies

Shakespeare employs the traditional comic conventions, such as stage tricks, stock characters, love stories, and happy endings, but he gives them his own personal stamp.

world of humans is made clear, however, when diagramed with a series of circles, triangles, and quadrangles.

Chapter Three: Shakespeare's Popular Romantic Comedies

making and excessive eating and drinking to discover greater satisfaction in reality and the fulfillment of their natural selves.

Chapter Four: Shakespeare's Final Plays

FOREWORD

*"'Tis the good reader that
makes the good book."*

Ralph Waldo Emerson

The story's bare facts are simple: The captain, an old and scarred seafarer, walks with a peg leg made of whale ivory. He relentlessly drives his crew to hunt the world's oceans for the great white whale that crippled him. After a long search, the ship encounters the whale and a fierce battle ensues. Finally the captain drives his harpoon into the whale, but the harpoon line catches the captain about the neck and drags him to his death.

A simple story, a straightforward plot—yet, since the 1851 publication of Herman Melville's *Moby-Dick*, readers and critics have found many meanings in the struggle between Captain Ahab and the whale. To some, the novel is a cautionary tale that depicts how Ahab's obsession with revenge leads to his insanity and death. Others believe that the whale represents the unknowable secrets of the universe and that Ahab is a tragic hero who dares to challenge fate by attempting to discover this knowledge. Perhaps Melville intended Ahab as a criticism of Americans' tendency to become involved in well-intentioned but irrational causes. Or did Melville model Ahab after himself, letting his fictional character express his anger at what he perceived as a cruel and distant god?

Although literary critics disagree over the meaning of *Moby-Dick*, readers do not need to choose one particular interpretation in order to gain an understanding of Melville's novel. Instead, by examining various analyses, they can gain numerous insights into the issues that lie under the surface of the basic plot. Studying the writings of literary critics can also aid readers in making their own assessments of *Moby-Dick* and other literary works and in developing analytical thinking skills.

The Greenhaven Literary Companion Series was created with these goals in mind. Designed for young adults, this unique anthology series provides an engaging and comprehensive introduction to literary analysis and criticism. The essays included in the Literary Companion Series are chosen for their accessibility to a young adult audience and are expertly edited in consideration of both the reading and comprehension levels of this audience. In addition, each essay is introduced by a concise summation that presents the contributing writer's main themes and insights. Every anthology in the Literary Companion Series contains a varied selection of critical essays that cover a wide time span and express diverse views. Wherever possible, primary sources are represented through excerpts from authors' notebooks, letters, and journals and through contemporary criticism.

Each title in the Literary Companion Series pays careful consideration to the historical context of the particular author or literary work. In-depth biographies and detailed chronologies reveal important aspects of authors' lives and emphasize the historical events and social milieu that influenced their writings. To facilitate further research, every anthology includes primary and secondary source bibliographies of articles and/or books selected for their suitability for young adults. These engaging features make the Greenhaven Literary Companion series ideal for introducing students to literary analysis in the classroom or as a library resource for young adults researching the world's great authors and literature.

Exceptional in its focus on young adults, the Greenhaven Literary Companion Series strives to present literary criticism in a compelling and accessible format. Every title in the series is intended to spark readers' interest in leading American and world authors, to help them broaden their understanding of literature, and to encourage them to formulate their own analyses of the literary works that they read. It is the editors' hope that young adult readers will find these anthologies to be true companions in their study of literature.

INTRODUCTION

The essays in this literary companion, *Readings on the Comedies*, provide teachers and students with a wide variety of information and opinion about William Shakespeare's comedies. Shakespeare wrote sixteen plays that are loosely referred to as his comedies, but aside from their generally happy endings there is much variation among them; the task of describing Shakespeare's plays is complicated because comedy in its tradition is a more varied form than, for example, tragedy.

This volume brings together a wide range of scholars and critics. Both American and British authors are represented. Selections cover more than a century of criticism, from Dowden in the 1880s to a twentieth-century feminist. Moreover, this volume includes essays by some of the most respected Shakespearean scholars and critics, including Northrop Frye, G.B. Harrison, Caroline F.E. Spurgeon, Helen Gardner, and Harold S. Wilson.

Many special features of this volume make research and literary criticism accessible and understandable. The annotated table of contents lets the reader identify the content of an essay quickly. Additional tools include a glossary of literary terms, a chronology of significant events in Shakespeare's life and in England during his lifetime, a list of Shakespeare's works, a thorough bibliography, and an extensive index.

A number of aids for understanding the author's ideas accompany each essay. The introduction clearly identifies the main points in the essay, which are highlighted within the essay by subheads. Footnotes identify uncommon references, define unfamiliar words that have special meanings, and explain Shakespeare's use of Elizabethan words appearing in excerpts. Most essays are complemented by boxed inserts that offer opposing or concurring views, illustrate an author's idea, or quote an entertaining passage. Taken together, these aids make the task of research manageable and satisfying.

WILLIAM SHAKESPEARE: A BIOGRAPHY

By today's standards, factual information about William Shakespeare is meager indeed; no diaries, journals, or letters survive to help biographers ascertain the author's personality or his opinions or beliefs. By Elizabethan standards, however, more records exist concerning the events in Shakespeare's life than one would expect for most untitled persons. Diligent scholars have located institutional records to identify Shakespeare's place of birth and upbringing and the essential events in his family life. They have unearthed records identifying some of his employment history and economic holdings. To supplement the records, scholars have turned to the text of his works and knowledge of Elizabethan history and beliefs to understand Shakespeare the man. Not surprisingly, interpretations differ.

BIRTH AND FAMILY

William Shakespeare was born in Stratford (today called Stratford-on-Avon) in Warwickshire, a county in the heart of England, on April 23 or 24, 1564. His birth date is presumed from the record of his baptism in Holy Trinity, the Stratford Church of England, on April 26; because so many children died in infancy, baptism usually occurred within two or three days of a child's birth. Shakespeare's mother, Mary Arden, came from an old county family. More genteel and prosperous than the Shakespeares, the Ardens provided their daughter with a dowry of land and money, which advanced the status of her husband, John Shakespeare, when the couple married in 1557. John Shakespeare was a wool dealer and glove maker in Stratford and, for a time, a prominent community leader and officeholder. He began public service as the town ale taster in 1557, and subsequently performed the offices of burgess, constable, town treasurer, alderman, and bailiff, or mayor. In the early 1580s, however,

John Shakespeare's financial troubles led to the loss of both his wealth and his governing positions.

William was the third of eight children born to Mary and John Shakespeare. Two daughters, Joan, christened in September 1558, and Margaret, christened in December 1562, died young. Four siblings were born after William reached adulthood: Gilbert, christened in October 1566; a second Joan, christened in 1569; Richard, christened in March 1573 or 1574; and Edmund, christened in 1580. Another daughter, Anne died at age eight.

EDUCATION

Though no school records exist, William likely attended public schools like the ones children throughout England attended. Typically, young children first spent a year in an elementary school for their letters (alphabet), numbers, and catechism (a book summarizing the basic principles of Christianity in question-and-answer form). After age seven, he probably attended grammar school at King's New School, where he received a rigorous education in classrooms taught by Oxford graduates. Simon Hunt and Thomas Jenkins, two of the headmasters during the years Shakespeare lived in Stratford, had advanced degrees.

Students were expected to be in their seats by six A.M. in the summer and seven A.M. in the winter for a school day that began and ended with Bible readings, psalm singing, and prayers. Students memorized Latin grammar and studied logic, Latin composition, and literature. The curriculum included the Roman dramatists Seneca, Terence, and Plautus; Renaissance religious texts; the Roman poets Horace, Virgil, and Ovid; the complete works of Dutch Renaissance scholar Erasmus; and the works of Roman orators, philosophers, and historians. Shakespeare, who drew from Ovid's *Metamorphoses* for his own plays and poems, likely remembered the classic from his grammar-school days. According to scholar and critic George R. Price, in *Reading Shakespeare's Plays*, "This education was at least comparable with a modern college major in classics." Years later, contemporary English playwright Ben Jonson disparagingly called Shakespeare's learning "small Latin and less Greek," but, by Jonson's standards, "much" learning would have meant a five-year study of Latin, ending with a master's degree.

Shakespeare's education, however, extended well beyond

the Stratford grammar school. Elizabethan law required regular attendance in the Protestant Church of England, so Shakespeare would have grown up listening to readings from the Bible and the *Book of Common Prayer*, the liturgical book of the Church of England. Scholars have counted in Shakespeare's plays allusions to forty books of the Bible and many references to the commandments, quotations from Psalms, and lines from the prayer book. In *Shakespeare the Man*, biographer A.L. Rowse calls Shakespeare a man educated in "the university of life." His plays display detailed knowledge of the entertainment, social mores, and culture of his native Warwickshire. Price says that we may

> be sure that the knowledge of hawking, hunting, and archery, of horses, dogs, and wild things, of peddlers, shepherds, and farm folk—this store of information in his plays and poems was not acquired only from books, but indicates a normal freedom to roam the countryside and enjoy himself.

Though he lived far from London, Shakespeare had at least a few opportunities to experience some of its cultural riches while a boy in Stratford. When John Shakespeare was bailiff, probably in 1569, troupes of players began to perform plays in the Guild Hall in Stratford. Though there are no records of John Shakespeare's attendance, as bailiff he would surely have brought his family to the entertainments. Traveling actors continued to stage plays in Stratford every year from the time William was five years old. In 1575 Shakespeare had another taste of London life when Queen Elizabeth I visited the earl of Leicester at his castle at Kenilworth, a few miles from Stratford. Called a progress, the queen's entourage included courtiers on horseback, coaches, hundreds of servants, and numerous carts hauling supplies. Country crowds gathered to watch the procession go by and perhaps hear a word from the queen. During the queen's stay—for nearly a month—crowds surrounded the castle to enjoy the pageants, water shows, and fireworks displays produced in the queen's honor.

EARLY MANHOOD

Though no record confirms this, Shakespeare left school at about age sixteen. When Shakespeare was eighteen years old, he married Anne Hathaway, eight years older than he. Biographers have made much of the fact that banns for the marriage were called only once, on December 1, 1582, rather than the usual three times; the inference is that church officials hurried the marriage because Anne was already pregnant. However, because Elizabethans considered betrothal (engagement) a binding agreement and in some instances the same as marriage, her pregnancy was less unusual than modern customs might consider it.

After the marriage, the couple lived with Shakespeare's family on Henley Street in Stratford. On May 26, 1583, their daughter Susanna was baptized; twenty months later the young couple had twins, baptized Hamnet and Judith on February 2, 1585. How this twenty-one-year-old man supported his family is unknown. An antiquarian and gossip, John Aubrey, born a decade after Shakespeare died, collected facts and anecdotes about public persons. In his journal, he says that someone told him that Shakespeare taught school and worked in his father's butcher shop. Since John Shakespeare had no butcher shop, Shakespeare either worked in someone else's butcher shop or his father's leather shop. Among the myths surrounding Shakespeare's life is the story that he was caught poaching deer in a park belonging to Sir Thomas Lucy of Charlecote, near Stratford. Historian Nicholas Rowe suggests that Shakespeare had to leave his business and family and take refuge in London to avoid prosecution, but the story has never been proved.

FIRST YEARS IN LONDON

The years 1585 to 1592 are called the "lost years" because no records of any kind document Shakespeare's movements or activities during the period. He probably went to London some time between 1585 and 1587, possibly joining up with a company of actors or striking out alone on foot. By one route, a man could walk to London in four days if he made twenty-five miles a day, lodging at inns along the way for a penny a night. In *Shakespeare: A Documentary Life*, Samuel Schoenbaum describes the city as Shakespeare would have found it on his arrival:

> The great city of contrasts spawned stately mansions and slum tenements, gardens and midden-heaped lanes. With the Court close to hand, it was the vital nerve-center for the professions, trade, and commerce, and the arts; London nourished the English Renaissance. Only in the metropolis could a playwright of genius forge a career for himself.

When Shakespeare came to London, attending plays was

the most popular form of entertainment for all classes, from poor students to aristocrats. London boasted several theaters: The first, built in 1576 by James Burbage, was called simply the Theatre, and the Fortune, the Swan, the Curtain, the Rose, and Blackfriars followed. The theaters were constructed with an open stage surrounded by uncovered space where a standing crowd viewed the performance. Three levels of covered seats surrounded the open space. Each theater had an all-male resident company of actors performing plays and competing with all the other theaters for popular approval. Female parts were played by boys usually recruited from the boys' choirs in the cathedrals. (Not until 1660 did a woman act onstage.) During the twelve days of Christmas, the companies performed plays in Queen Elizabeth's court to entertain royal guests; for those performances, painted scenery identified the settings in which elaborately clad actors performed. Throughout the year, traveling troupes drawn from the companies also performed in towns and cities outside London.

One story goes that Shakespeare began his career by holding patrons' horses outside the theater; another says that he began as a prompter's attendant. He may have done both jobs for a short time and then advanced to acting before becoming the company's writer. Though attending plays was popular London entertainment, many moralists complained that the jokes were too bawdy and that young men neglected their church duties in favor of playgoing. Consequently, society looked on actors as riffraff at worst and men of questionable reputation at best. Price comments: "When Shakespeare became an actor, he must have deeply grieved the heart of his father and mother, and he surely gave himself cause for extreme discomfort at times." John Aubrey mentions no misgivings, however, and writes: "He was a handsome, well-shap't man: very good company, and of a very readie and pleasant smoothe Witt."

Because Shakespeare was an outsider in London, a country man who lacked the sophistication and easy manners of the Cambridge and Oxford University men, he studied the ways of a gentleman, found a mentor, and read widely. Shakespeare looked to Cambridge-educated playwright Christopher Marlowe, who was the same age but who preceded Shakespeare in skillfully combining drama with poetry. In many plays throughout his career, Shakespeare pays tribute to Marlowe, though ultimately he eclipsed Marlowe as a dramatist. Shakespeare's romantic nature was influenced by the works of two English poets: Sir Philip Sidney's sonnets and *The Arcadia*, a prose romance, and Edmund Spenser's *The Faerie Queene*, an allegory glorifying England and the queen. Shakespeare, who loved his country and her history, also read the *Chronicles* of Raphael Holinshed, a historian who came to London early in Elizabeth's reign, and the works of historian Edward Hall, who wrote about England's past royal families. Shakespeare borrowed plots from these works for many of his plays and used poetic techniques like those of Sidney and Spenser.

Records show that Shakespeare had already made his mark as a playwright by 1592. His early plays—*The Tragedy of Titus Andronicus*; *Henry VI, Parts I, II,* and *III; The Comedy of Errors*; and *Richard III*—mimic the dramatic forms laid out by the Roman playwrights he studied in grammar school. His popularity elicited a comment in a 1592 journal left by Robert Greene, a popular Cambridge-educated playwright who died soon afterward. In his *Groatsworth of Wit*, Greene, complaining that the professional actors had forsaken university men like him, specifically attacked Shakespeare:

> Yes trust them not: for there is an upstart Crow, beautified with our feathers, that with his *Tygers hart wrapt in a Players hyde,*[1] supposes he is as well able to bombast out a blanke verse as the best of you: and beeing an absolute *Johannes fac totum,*[2] is in his owne conceit the onely Shake-scene in a countrey.

SHAKESPEARE AS A POET

About the time Greene's comment appeared, a plague spread through London, lasting through 1593, and the lord mayor ordered the theaters closed. Without theater work, Shakespeare made his first appeal to the reading public. He had wanted to be a poet, which he considered a noble occupation; he thought acting and writing plays were merely means to support a family. None of his plays, which were written for live performance, had been published by 1592. On April 18, 1593, the printer Richard Field obtained license to publish Shakespeare's poem *Venus and Adonis* and on May 9, 1594, license to publish another poem, *Lucrece*.

Shakespeare also wrote a series of 154 sonnets, which

1. a parody on Shakespeare's line from *Henry VI*, which says, "O tiger's heart wrapt in a woman's hide!"   2. a "John Do-everything," a jack-of-all-trades

celebrate a beautiful young man and express powerful passion for a mysterious dark lady at whose hands the poet suffers greatly. Since neither the young man nor the dark lady is named, critics have gone to great lengths to try to verify their identity. Most critics conclude that the twenty sonnets dedicated to the young man and the many others that celebrate him in glowing terms refer to the earl of Southampton, who had become Shakespeare's patron. No less critical energy has been devoted to determining whether or not the sonnets are autobiographical. Biographer A.L. Rowse, who thinks they are, agrees that the young man is the earl of Southampton and identifies the dark lady as Emilia Bassano, daughter of an Italian musician in the queen's court.

THE TURNING POINT IN SHAKESPEARE'S CAREER

In 1594 Shakespeare turned away from sonnet writing—he also turned thirty in April that year. With the end of the plague, the earl of Southampton's patronage ended, and with the reopening of the theaters, Shakespeare established himself with an acting company. By the summer of 1594, a group of actors formerly with other companies had formed a company under the patronage of Henry Lord Hunsdon, lord chamberlain to the queen, calling themselves Lord Chamberlain's Men. They played at various theaters—the Theatre, the Curtain, the Swan—before settling at the Globe. Among the company's permanent members were Henry Condell, John Heminge, Shakespeare, Richard Burbage (son of the Theatre's builder James Burbage), William Sly, and Will Kempe. Burbage, the famous tragedian, and Kempe, the famous comedian, played leading roles in plays Shakespeare wrote specifically for their talents. From then on, Shakespeare was completely involved in the theater: He wrote for the company, acted in the plays, shared in the profits, and eventually became one of the owners of the Globe theater. While in London, he worked hard and played little; he lived during those years as a lodger in a quiet room near the playhouse where he could write without interruption.

Shakespeare's first success as a playwright came between 1593 and 1598. *Love's Labour's Lost*, probably the only play with an entirely original plot, portrays current social and political life. Shakespeare's style in his early comedies shows evidence of the influence of John Lyly, who wrote eight comedies between 1580 and 1592 that were enthusiastically welcomed at the court of Queen Elizabeth. Adapting themes from Greek mythology, Lyly wrote in euphuistic style; that is, with artificial dialogues rich with repartee and wordplay, musical lyrics, and elaborate imagery. Critics have called several of Shakespeare's early plays lyrical because they contain passages of beautiful description and passionate feelings, among them *The Two Gentlemen from Verona.* With *A Midsummer Night's Dream,* Shakespeare had already gone beyond Lyly in creating a more inventive plot and more interesting characters from the fairy world. *The Taming of the Shrew* and *The Tragedy of Romeo and Juliet* exemplify other characteristics of his early plays; both have long explanatory speeches written in stiff verse and intricate plots that imitate Marlowe and the plays Shakespeare studied in grammar school.

Besides writing comedy during this period, Shakespeare also wrote history plays about England's past kings: *Richard II*; *Henry IV, Parts I* and *II*; *Henry V*; and *King John.* The plays about Henry IV were especially popular with audiences who loved the humorous character of the knight Falstaff. Falstaff's unrestrained indulgence in sensual pleasures, his love of telling big lies, and his own laziness are set against great good humor and consistent wit. Sidney Lee says, "Shakespeare's purely comic power culminated in Falstaff; he may be claimed as the most humorous figure in literature." After Falstaff disappeared as a character in the history plays, Queen Elizabeth requested that Shakespeare write another in which Falstaff falls in love. Shakespeare complied with *The Merry Wives of Windsor,* but in this play Falstaff is the butt, not the creator, of humor. During this period, Shakespeare also wrote the comedies *Much Ado About Nothing* and *The Merchant of Venice,* both of which have two stories or two threads of interest.

Shakespeare received praise from many sources for his early works. Among the most notable were comments by Francis Meres, a learned Cambridge graduate, who in *Palladis Tamia: Wit's Treasury* called Shakespeare the greatest man of letters. He says:

> So the sweet witty soul of Ovid lives in mellifluous and honeytongued Shakespeare, witness his *Venus and Adonis,* his *Lucrece,* his sugared *Sonnets* among his private friends, etc.

> As Plautus and Seneca are accounted the best for Comedy and Tragedy among the Latins: so Shakespeare among the English is the most excellent in both kinds for the stage. . . .

As Epius Stolo said, that the Muses would speak with Plautus' tongue if they would speak Latin: so I say that the Muses would speak with Shakespeare's fine filled phrase, if they would speak English.

But Stratford remained the center of Shakespeare's personal life, the place to which he returned each summer and in which he invested his money. In 1596 and 1597, Shakespeare was occupied with three significant family matters. First, in August 1596 Shakespeare's son Hamnet died; with the death of his eleven-year-old son, Shakespeare lost hope of perpetuating the family in his name. Anne Shakespeare was forty and could not be expected to have another child. Shakespeare expressed his grief in the play he was writing at the time, *King John*:

Grief fills the room up of my absent child,
Lies in his bed, walks up and down with me,
Puts on his pretty looks, repeats his words,
Remembers me of all his gracious parts,
Stuffs out his vacant garments with his form. (act 3, scene 4)

Second, even though he had no son to carry on the family name, Shakespeare pressed to obtain the title and coat of arms of a gentleman, a status evidently important to him. So that he could be considered born the son of a gentleman, Shakespeare applied and paid cash for a grant in the name of his father. On October 20, 1596, Garter King of Arms William Dethick issued a coat of arms with a falcon and a silver spear and declared Shakespeare a gentleman by birth. Today, the coat of arms is displayed on the Shakespeare monument at Stratford. Finally, in May 1597, Shakespeare purchased New Place, a large house in the center of Stratford with two barns and two orchards and gardens. Before he was thirty-five years old, Shakespeare had achieved the status of gentleman, property owner, and playwright, but he had lost his only male heir.

THE GLOBE THEATER

In 1597, James Burbage, who had built the Theatre in 1576, died, and Lord Chamberlain's Men lost their lease. About the same time, Puritans increased their opposition to what they perceived as the immorality of the city theaters. The Lord Chamberlain's Men found backing to dismantle the Theatre, move the boards across the Thames from London's city center, and build the Globe away from the Puritans. By this time,

Shakespeare had acquired enough wealth to buy one-tenth of the shares in the new theater.

The Globe outshone its competitors; it held two thousand spectators and was equipped with a bigger stage, a cellerage for graves and ghosts, a curtained space for intimate and surprise scenes, and a balcony. The audience was closer to the players, and the players had more flexibility to move quickly from scene to scene. *Henry V*, in which Shakespeare played the part of the chorus, anticipates the Globe. In the prologue, he refers to the new theater with excitement:

> A kingdom for a stage, princes to act
> And monarchs to behold the swelling scene! . . .
>   Can this cockpit[3] hold
> The vasty fields of France? Or may we cram
> Within this wooden O[4] the very casques[5]
> That did affright the air at Agincourt?[6]

In the epilogue, Shakespeare displays a characteristically humble attitude toward himself, writing:

> Thus far, with rough and all-unable pen,
> Our bending[7] author hath pursued the story,
> In little room[8] confining mighty men,
> Mangling by starts[9] the full course of their glory.

Though he himself may have been self-assured, he speaks as a humble gentleman throughout his works, self-deprecatingly calling himself "a worthless boat," "inferior far" to Marlowe. Others found this attitude charming and Shakespeare soon gained a reputation for congeniality.

OUTPOURING OF COMEDIES AND TRAGEDIES

After 1598 Shakespeare's comedies and tragedies appeared quickly one after another. He turned from English history to Roman history and used *Lives*, by Greek philosopher and biographer Plutarch, as a source for plots. *The Tragedy of Julius Caesar*, dated 1599, explores Brutus's character and motives. In addition, Shakespeare wrote three comedies to suit Will Kempe's talents. Besides *The Merry Wives of Windsor*, Kempe starred in *As You Like It* and *Twelfth Night*. *As You Like It* demonstrates many kinds of love and ends with four marriages. *Twelfth Night*, or *What You Will*, Shakespeare's most musical play, blends serious themes with

3. playhouse   4. the playhouse   5. the actual helmets   6. the French village where Henry V defeated a larger French army   7. bowing   8. the theater   9. marring the story by telling it in fragments

comedy. The title comes from its performance before the queen during Twelfth Night of 1599–1600.

After 1600 Shakespeare wrote his greatest tragedies, distinguished from the earlier works by more subtle language and deeper spirit. *Hamlet* and *Othello* came first. Shakespeare scholar and critic G.B. Harrison says that *"Hamlet* is in every way the most interesting play ever written"; for nearly four hundred years, it has challenged actors and scholars to interpret Hamlet's character. *Othello*, a unified and focused play, portrays evil in the character of Iago as he exploits Othello's jealousy and Desdemona's innocence to destroy them and their love.

The opening of the Globe marked a new phase in Shakespeare's reputation and art. Firmly established as the leading dramatist in London, Shakespeare's art became more refined and subtle. Price says, "Art has replaced artifice. The style has become so fully expressive of the thought that audience and readers are unconscious of the poet's devices." Shakespeare, who was interested in the workings of human character, objectively displays his characters' minds in the actions and speeches he wrote for them. The soliloquies of Brutus, Hamlet, and Iago, for example, lay bare their intentions and their very souls.

Among his friends and fellow playwrights, Shakespeare had a reputation for writing headlong with little attention to revision. Aubrey reports playwright Ben Jonson's opinion of Shakespeare's method of writing: "He was wont to say that he never blotted out a line in his life. Sayd Ben Johnson, I wish he had blotted out a thousand." In the annual Shakespeare Lecture at the British Academy in 1972, M.M. Mahood acknowledges the faults in the texts. Mahood says, "Shakespeare's plays abound in loose ends, false starts, confusions, and anomalies of every kind." Many of the faults occur in the comedies; for example, in *Taming of the Shrew*, the characters of Sly and the Hostess disappear from the play.

Though Shakespeare continued to write, the period from 1598 to 1604 brought significant personal diversions. In September 1601 his father died in Stratford. The following May, Shakespeare bought 107 acres of farmland in Old Stratford for £320, and in September a cottage on Walkers Street. On March 24, 1603, Queen Elizabeth, who had actively supported the Lord Chamberlain's Men, died. James I succeeded her, took over the company, renamed it the King's

Men, and supported the players even more avidly than the queen had, making them an official part of his court, doubling their salaries, and increasing their annual court appearances from three to thirteen. In addition, he gave them license to perform in any town or university. These changes required Shakespeare to pay greater attention to the approval of two audiences, the court and the Globe. Shakespeare's increase in income allowed him to invest £440 in tithes in parishes in Stratford and surrounding towns, investments that brought additional income of £60 a year.

THE KING'S MEN

From 1604 to 1608, as a member of the King's Men, Shakespeare's art changed again. He wrote two transitional comedies in which he experimented with techniques to work out dramatic problems. *All's Well That Ends Well*, an uneven play seldom performed, involves a young woman who tricks a man into becoming her husband. *Measure for Measure*, called a problem play because the plot poorly fits the theme, concerns a woman who compromises her chastity to save her brother. In *Shakespeare: The Complete Works*, G.B. Harrison calls it "one of Shakespeare's unpleasant plays"; other critics have spoken of it less charitably.

After 1604 Shakespeare's tragedies probed even more deeply into the minds of their heroes. *The Tragedy of King Lear* was first performed in King James's court during the Christmas holidays of 1606. Critics regard *Lear* as Shakespeare's greatest play, though not his most popular. The play has a double plot; Lear suffers at the hands of his daughters and Gloucester at the hands of his son. Both die, but each has one child who remains loyal. The play's greatness lies in the psychological depth of Lear's character and the stark reality of both human nature and nature's elements.

Shakespeare wrote *Macbeth* in 1606, as a tribute to James I on the occasion of a state visit from the king of Denmark. The play is set in Scotland, James's home before he became king of England. The good character Banquo is a member of the Scottish Stuart family, ancestors of James. Shakespeare further honored the king, who was interested in witchcraft, by incorporating the three witches into the play. Though he did not find King James I an honorable man, Shakespeare fulfilled his duty to the king upon whose patronage he depended. Like *Lear*, *Macbeth* reaches below the rational level into the subconscious, where primitive impulses lie in recesses of the mind; the tragic Macbeth and Lady Macbeth, having plotted the murder of King Duncan to put Macbeth on the throne, see their plot undone and suffer mental anguish before they too die.

After the four great tragedies, Shakespeare returned to Plutarch's *Lives* as a source for three more. *The Tragedy of Antony and Cleopatra* picks up the story of Roman history where *Julius Caesar* left off. *The Tragedy of Coriolanus* is a political play in which Shakespeare exposes the weakness of all manner of politicians and presents the crowd as a fickle mob in a tone more bitter than in his exposé of the crowd in *Julius Caesar*. *Timon of Athens*, an unfinished play, tells about an ancient Greek mentioned briefly in Plutarch's *Lives*.

During this period, when Shakespeare wrote one or more plays a year and kept a busy schedule of productions at court and at the Globe, little is known of his personal life. His daughter Susanna married a well-known medical doctor from Stratford named John Hall on June 5, 1607. In September 1608 his mother, Mary Arden Shakespeare, died, and in October 1608 Shakespeare was named godfather to the son of Stratford alderman Henry Walker, whose son was named William in honor of Shakespeare.

In 1609 a respected publisher, Thomas Thorpe, published without Shakespeare's knowledge a book entitled *Shakespeare's Sonnets: Never Before Imprinted*. Since no copyright laws existed at the time, any person with a manuscript in hand could register it, publish it, and become its owner. Two factors indicate that Shakespeare had no part in the publication: The dedication appearing under the title was by the publisher, a common practice when an author was not involved; and the volume contained numerous errors and even missing words, unlike the editions of the two poems that Shakespeare had prepared for printing. After Thorpe's edition, the sonnets were not reprinted until 1640; some critics think a displeased Shakespeare took measures to prevent further circulation in 1609.

THE FINAL PERIOD

After the outpouring of tragedies, Shakespeare's art changed again; in part because of changes in theater ownership and attendance. Blackfriars, a private theater owned by Richard Burbage, had been leased to a boys' company. Burbage,

Shakespeare, and other actors bought back the lease and began performances there for upper-class audiences more like those at court. Blackfriars audiences liked new plays, while the public audiences at the Globe preferred old favorites. This situation suited Shakespeare, who could try new plays that were neither comedies nor tragedies at Blackfriars. Some critics have called the new plays romances; others, tragi-comedies. These plays express themes of reunion after long separation followed by reconciliation and forgiveness. The plots revolve around children lost and then found, divided parents brought together, or an innocent person threatened but retrieved. Before characters find a haven, they have been through storms and stress, encountered evil, or endured suffering. Rowse says: "For all their happy endings, these plays have an atmosphere full of suggestion and symbol, suffused with tears."

Shakespeare wrote four plays in this new form. *Pericles* is a transitional play, portions of which appear to have been written by a second playwright. After experimenting with *Pericles*, Shakespeare wrote *Cymbeline*, probably in 1610, a melodrama about an innocent girl who flees mistreatment and encounters a host of crises before she is reunited with her repentant husband. *The Winter's Tale*, written in 1610 or 1611, is a moving tale of wrongs committed by one generation and reconciled in the next.

The Tempest, a play written for James I to celebrate a court wedding, is Shakespeare's farewell to the theater. This fairy tale about a magician and his beautiful daughter ends with the reconciliation of two generations. G.B. Harrison praises *The Tempest*:

> Shakespeare has finally achieved complete mastery over words in the blank-verse form. This power is shown throughout the play, but particularly in some of Prospero's great speeches, ... or in his farewell to his art. There is in these speeches a kind of organ note not hitherto heard. Shakespeare's thought was as deep as in his tragedies, but now he was able to express each thought with perfect meaning and its own proper harmony.

Prospero, the magician of *The Tempest*, recounts his tricks in words that some critics think apply aptly to Shakespeare. After cataloging the marvels he has conjured up over the years, from raging storms to corpses rising from the grave to a dimmed sun, he announces, "this rough magic / I here abjure. . . . I'll break my staff, / Bury it certain fathoms in the earth, / And . . . I'll drown my book."[10] Shakespeare's only play after this farewell was *Henry VIII*, a history full of pageantry, music, and ceremony. During the June 29, 1613, performance of *Henry VIII*, a spark from a cannon set the thatch roof of the Globe alight and burned the building to the ground. Though the Globe was rebuilt by 1614, there is reason to believe that the players' books and many of Shakespeare's original manuscripts were lost in the fire.

From 1612 on, Shakespeare divided his time between Stratford and London, and once went to Parliament to lobby for better roads between the two cities. In 1612 his brother Gilbert died, followed by his brother Richard the next year. Shakespeare spent 1614 and 1615 in Stratford enjoying his retirement and his daughters, but information about his wife, Anne, seems to be nonexistent. The parish register of Holy Trinity shows that on February 10, 1616, Shakespeare's younger daughter, Judith, was married to Thomas Quiney, the son of Shakespeare's old friend Richard Quiney. On March 25, 1616, while he was in fine health, Shakespeare made a will. He left a dowry and additional money to Judith and all lands and houses to his older daughter, Susanna, and her heirs. He left his wife to the care of his daughters and willed her the next-best bed, reasoning that Susanna and her husband needed the bigger better one. To his sister, he left money for clothes and the home on Henley Street. He gave small amounts of money to friends and money for rings to fellow actors of the King's Men. And he left money for the poor in Stratford. A month later, after a trip to London, he suddenly became ill and died on April 23, 1616, at fifty-two. As he lay dying, the chapel bell knelled for the passing of his soul, for the man for whom love was the center of the universe and the central subject of his many works.

During his lifetime, Shakespeare made no effort to publish his works, other than the two long poems. His plays belonged to the members of the theater company, who sold individual plays for publication when readers requested them in the early 1600s. In 1623—the year Anne Hathaway Shakespeare died—two actors from the King's Men, Henry Condell and John Heminge, collected Shakespeare's plays and published them, in what is known as the First Folio, and they have been in print ever since. Some skeptics, doubting

10. of magic spells

Shakespeare's genius, have speculated that his works were
written by Francis Bacon or others. But such theories are advanced by the uninformed. As Price says: "No first-rate
scholar has ever accepted the evidence offered by the Baco-
nians or others who argue that Shakespeare did not write
the dramas that his fellow-actors, Heminge and Condell,
published as his."

CHAPTER 1

The Spirit and Development of Shakespeare's Comedies

READINGS ON
THE COMEDIES

Shakespeare's Comedies Are Playful

John Jay Chapman

John Jay Chapman argues that in his comedies Shakespeare creates a world of freedom and happiness and, above all, safety. Capturing the spirit of this world, especially magical in the most lighthearted plays, *As You Like It*, *A Midsummer Night's Dream*, *Twelfth Night*, and *The Taming of the Shrew*, is a challenge for actors. Chapman suggests that thinking of these comedies as children's plays may help modern readers retain the appropriate attitude of humor and playfulness. John Jay Chapman was an American literary critic, translator, essayist, playwright, and poet of the late nineteenth and early twentieth centuries. Writing shortly after the catastrophic violence of World War I, Chapman's appreciation of Shakespeare's safe world is especially poignant.

Whenever there seemed to be a chance that the Germans might win the war, I was haunted by momentary visions of the past,—that part of the past whose spirit was threatened,—the spirit of joy, relaxation, and dreamy happiness. I saw, as in a flash, Falstaff sitting on the tavern bench in the sun and unbuttoning his belt after dinner, Toby Belch going to burn more sack[1] and swearing it was not late yet. I heard Bottom calling for an almanac, and boasting that he would do it in 'Ercles' vein, Audrey asking Touchstone, "What is honest? Is it a good thing?" and Grumio describing his master's wedding-journey with the Shrew. Such scenes from Shakespeare, and fragmentary memories of the man himself and of his age, would pass by in my mind as if they were the thing attacked by this whole German onslaught. . . .

1. wine

From John Jay Chapman, *A Glance Toward Shakespeare* (Boston: Atlantic Monthly Press, 1922).

This war-experience gave me a new clue to English literature. A sense of personal safety is one of the elements that is felt all through English letters. It is the climate in which the English genius, which is the genius for happiness, developed. How similar in spirit is all the joyous part of English fiction, from Chaucer to Surtees's sporting books! There is the same glow in "Twelfth Night" that there is in "Pickwick Papers." The rapture of mere existence is in all this work. It has been made without intention. Intention is a damage to it, as we see often in Dickens, and always in George Eliot; and the substratum of it is common life, good-humor, observation, courage, an indeterminate way of living, and an abundance of force. The English write as they live—in the moment. . . .

Ever since Shakespeare's day, his hand is to be seen everywhere in the fiction and humor of England. . . . They are gay people, the English, and except when they try to be clever, are the cleverest people in the world. Ebulliency, enthusiasm, and the absence of literary pose are the great features of English literature. If you cast your eye over the whole panorama, the low life in it appears to be better done than the high life. The reason of this may be that great writers are almost always men of the people; and, as they thoroughly know the people, they describe them to the life; but they make guesses as to the aristocracy.

In Shakespeare, both the high life and the low life are equally convincing when we read the plays to ourselves; but on the modern stage a very strange thing happens. the low comedy is apt to be heavy and conscientious. . . .

COMEDIES ARE HARD TO ACT WELL

As for high comedy, Garrick[2] used to say that in tragedy he could always bring down the house, no matter in what mood he stepped upon the boards, whether he had a headache or felt sick or indifferent. "But comedy—comedy is a serious business!" This is no doubt a universal experience with actors; and Shakespeare's comedies, each of which is so different in spirit, in tempo, in coloring from the rest, are probably the most difficult of all comedies to act well. "As You Like It," for instance, is a water-color sketch—there is little drama in it. Rosalind's repartees cannot be gilded. Touch-

2. David, actor and producer of Shakespeare's plays

stone's soliloquies will not bear a frame. The set speeches in "As You Like It"—as for instance, "Now, my co-mates and brothers-in-exile," or Oliver's two long speeches describing how he was rescued by his brothers from the sucked and hungry lioness—cannot be informed with passion; and yet they must be beautiful. They say that Mozart's music is the most difficult of all music to play—it is so perfect and yet so delicate. You must live yourself back into the world as it was before the French Revolution if you would play Mozart correctly. No one has the time to do this, and therefore Mozart cannot be played. In like manner, "As You Like It" is apt to drag. We have all become heavy-fisted nowadays, and we pound our texts. Where poetry, foolery, and philosophy meet, as they do in these sylvan scenes,—all of them tinged with a world that has long ago disappeared,—we are like burglars dancing a minuet. Perhaps, instead of bewailing the vanishment of the old English stage, we ought rather to wonder at the genius of Shakespeare, which has so long kept alive the art of imaginative, happy badinage,[3] during a century whose social life has been growing ever more and more unimaginative, graceless, and practical.

In giving one of the lesser comedies, the mood of the piece is harder to find, and its keynote harder to sound, than in the great ones. The "Merchant of Venice" expounds itself like a tragedy, and is so various, interesting, and full of passion that it is easy to act. The lighter plays present the heavier problems. In "Much Ado About Nothing" the plot is more serious and the whole humor and intrigue of the piece more sprightly than in "As You Like It." How shall we find, how hit upon that talisman, that "Open, Sesame," which shall show the inner life of each of these delicate masterpieces? The plays themselves must teach us. They were not created, nor have they been sustained, by any academy. We have only tradition, personal feeling, and experience to guide us.

The "Taming of the Shrew" has still another, and very different, temperament of its own. It is a very subtle, quizzical, humane, philosophic piece of nonsense. In the "Midsummer Night's Dream" you have, again, a region of fancy so utterly different from all these last-mentioned plays, that it seems as if it must have been made by another hand. It is steeped in the peculiar atmosphere of the world's fairyland, and seems

3. light, playful banter

to be a whole literature in itself. "Twelfth Night" is, again, a new universe. It is the best light comedy in the world and swims like a ruddy planet, bearing the inhabitants of the Golden Age. It is a saturnalia[4] of good feeling, leisure, wit, and amusement in which both high and low revel by day and night. Each of these comedies is a unity, and resounds harmoniously when its chords are touched; but the works must not be attacked with vigor, and the keynotes of them must be rather listened for and imagined than struck.

THE CHILD'S SPIRIT IN COMEDIES

Perhaps the sophisticated modern person can best approach Shakespeare's comedies by thinking of them as child's plays, things beneath his serious notice and therefore to be humored. Otherwise the casket scene in the "Merchant of Venice" will disgust him. It is, indeed, probable that the folklore and fairy tales of the world are kept alive by the infant population of the world, and that no man, who first discovers these things after he is grown up, will be apt to find much meaning in them. The ancients lived on nursery tales; but every man, even then, had learned these tales first in the nursery. And I suspect that to-day, if the myths and auld wives' stories should die out of our nurseries, they would die out altogether; and then, of course, there would be nothing for the learned to talk about except politics, economics, eugenics, and ethnology—subjects which deal with mankind in masses, and take the individual for granted. To the poet there are no Masses, but only men. He speaks to each one of us severally. The poets throw open the windows and let in currents that carry life, awaken energy, and make men sensitive, powerful, wise, eloquent, capable of seeing the world,—I will not say as it is, for no man has seen that,—but more nearly as it is than men ever can see it without the light of poetry.

---

4. a Roman seven-day festival

Shakespeare's Comedies Are Progressively More Masterful

G.B. Harrison

G.B. Harrison divides Shakespeare's plays into four periods and argues that in each period the language becomes more subtle, the characters more fully drawn, and the ideas more complex. In the Early Period, according to Harrison, the language is stiff and decorated with excessive rhetorical devices and imagery. The plots are well worked out, but the characters are superficial. In the Balanced Period, Harrison says, Shakespeare better matches dialogue to scene, and characters speak in a more natural rhythm. Focusing on a few characters, Shakespeare makes their motivation clearer and feelings deeper. During the Overflowing Period, Shakespeare wrote the great tragedies, but no comedies. In the Final Period, Harrison says that Shakespeare achieves balance between thought and language, mastering the expression needed for his complex meaning. G.B. Harrison, a Shakespearean scholar who taught in London and Canada before teaching at the University of Michigan at Ann Arbor, edited a popular edition of the complete works, wrote numerous critical studies of Shakespeare's poetry and plays, and published works on Elizabethan England.

Shakespeare learned his craft in the best of schools, the theater itself. . . . At first Shakespeare copied his masters, but he soon learned to develop his own techniques, and to the end of his career he was constantly experimenting. The changes in his style are indeed so noticeable that his plays can be approximately dated by style alone.

Shakespeare's poetic style can conveniently be divided

into four periods: Early, Balanced, Overflowing, and Final.

To the Early Period belong... *Love's Labor's Lost*, *The Two Gentlemen of Verona*, *The Comedy of Errors*, *The Taming of the Shrew*, *Romeo and Juliet*, and *A Midsummer Night's Dream*. Plays of this period have certain common characteristics. The plots are, on the whole, well worked out; but except in *Romeo and Juliet* the characterization is usually superficial, the psychology seldom subtle, and the dialogue inclined to be stiff, artificial, and overlong. There is an abundance of such rhetorical devices as repetition of phrase, question, exclamation, alliteration, and excess of punning and word play. . . .

There is an excess of poetic imagery, often self-conscious, elaborate, and clever rather than illuminating. Thus in *A Midsummer Night's Dream* (act 3, scene 2) Helena tearfully protests against Hermia's unkindness, so cruel after their schoolgirl affection:

> Oh, is it all forgot?
> All school days' friendship, childhood innocence?
> We, Hermia, like two artificial[1] gods,
> Have with our needles created both one flower,
> Both on one sampler,[2] sitting on one cushion,
> Both warbling of one song, both in one key—
> As if our hands, our sides, voices, and minds
> Had been incorporate.[3] So we grew together,
> Like to a double cherry, seeming parted
> But yet a union in partition—
> Two lovely berries molded on one stem.
> So, with two seeming bodies, but one heart,
> Two of the first, like coats in heraldry,
> Due but to one, and crownèd with one crest.[4]
> And will you rent our ancient love asunder,
> To join with men in scorning your poor friend?

The imagery of the double cherries and the coat of arms is altogether too elaborate to illustrate the simple idea of long-established friendship, unless—as is very possible—Shakespeare is here deliberately parodying a failing common in his own early work.

Rhyme is very common, verse lines are monotonously regular, stresses even, and verse and sentence usually end together. At first Shakespeare composed his speeches line by line as if he were laying bricks one on top of the other; and

1. creative 2. piece of embroidery 3. in one body 4. an elaborate metaphor, from heraldry, meaning two bodies with a single heart

he had an excessive taste for puns. . . .

At this stage in his career, Shakespeare did not always have much to say, but he said it at great length, and all the time he was experimenting with the uses of words. He was more a conscious artist than an instinctive dramatist. Nevertheless the artificiality of Shakespeare's verse often has charm, and at times even considerable power. . . .

From the first, however, Shakespeare's comic dialogue in prose was easy and mature. Bottom, Quince, and company in *A Midsummer Night's Dream* are as fully developed as any of the later clowns, such as Dogberry and Verges in *Much Ado about Nothing*, the gravedigger in *Hamlet*, or Stephano and Trinculo in *The Tempest*.

The Early Period passed gradually into the Balanced Period. At all times Shakespeare wrote magnificent passages of poetry, but in the early plays the set piece is noticeably finer than its surroundings; in the later plays the whole effect is more even, and the dialogue is less concerned with fine sayings than with what is immediately appropriate to the scene. The main difference between the Early and the Balanced styles is that as Shakespeare's experience deepened, his power of expression grew. Speeches are now written as a whole, in one sweep; run-on lines become more common, and though the formal pattern of the verse remains, the stresses no longer tick like an ill-balanced grandfather clock.

Early and Balanced merge in *The Merchant of Venice*, which is perhaps the first play where Shakespeare is completely master of his craft. There are few long speeches of poetry for its own sake. The casket scene where Bassanio wins Portia (act 3, scene 2) is a little drawn-out, but the effect is deliberate and intentional, and leads up to the lyric moment when Portia gives herself to Bassanio. The verse has become easier, the rhythm more varied, the power and emotion deeper. . . .

The characterization also is elaborate and successful. . . . There are three principal methods by which character can be shown: by what is said of a man by his friends, and not less important by his enemies; by what he says of himself, and how he says it; and by his own actions. Description of a character is the most obvious method. Ben Jonson in his plays made a feature of elaborate descriptions, which mainly occur just before the person appears. Shakespeare, however, was much more subtle. He seldom wrote long or elaborate descriptions of his characters. Instead he built up a character stroke by stroke, revealing each trait as it was needed. . . .

The Balanced Period lasted . . . roughly from 1597 to 1603, and includes *Henry V, Much Ado about Nothing, The Merry Wives of Windsor, As You Like It, Julius Caesar, Hamlet, Twelfth Night, Troilus and Cressida, Measure for Measure,* and *All's Well That Ends Well.* During this time Shakespeare's own experience of life was deepening and his power of expression expanding. By the end he could write speeches which were not only full of the subtlest characterization but, by their choice of vocabulary and rhythm, could express the whole nature of the speaker. . . .

The growth of dramatic power can be seen also in Shakespeare's increasing knowledge of human character and a certain change in his interest and point of view. In his early plays, he tended rather to see the whole story objectively. Some characters naturally were more important, but each was treated alike. From about 1599, for the next six or seven years—that is, from *As You Like It* and *Julius Caesar* to *Lear* and *Macbeth*—Shakespeare often selected one or two characters in the play for special treatment, so that we see not only what happens to them, but also the working and development of their minds. . . .

Soliloquy—where a character left to himself reveals his own mind in a direct speech to the audience—was not a new device. Shakespeare and indeed all Elizabethan dramatists used it frequently, but in his earlier plays soliloquy was used mainly for three purposes: to give necessary information of the speaker's intentions, as when, at the end of the first scene of *A Midsummer Night's Dream,* Helena explains that she will tell Demetrius of Hermia's flight; or to reveal that the speaker is playing a part and is not what he seems, as when Richard of Gloucester gloats over his treachery to his brother Clarence; or as an excuse for an outburst of sheer poetry, as when Juliet waiting for Romeo breaks into a lyric ecstasy on night and love. . . .

The interest is not so much in what may ultimately happen as in the working and development of the personality of the speaker. It is as if Shakespeare for a while was more interested in men's motives than in their actions.

When he came to write *Lear,* Shakespeare was again experimenting with language. By this time his thoughts and feelings were coming too thick and powerful for balanced expression. He entered into an Overflowing Period.[5] . . .

At the end of his career, Shakespeare reached a Final Period, shown particularly in his last play, *The Tempest*, where he achieved perfect mastery and balance between thought, phrase, and meaning. It is seen in such a speech as Prospero's farewell to his art:

> Ye elves of hills, brooks, standing lakes, and groves,
> And ye that on the sands with printless foot[6]
> Do chase the ebbing Neptune[7] and do fly him
> When he comes back; you demipuppets[8] that
> By moonshine do the green sour[9] ringlets[10] make,
> Whereof the ewe not bites; and you whose pastime
> Is to make midnight mushrooms[11] that rejoice
> To hear the solemn curfew,[12] by whose aid—
> Weak masters though ye be—I have bedimmed
> The noontide sun, called forth the mutinous winds,
> And twixt the green sea and the azured vault[13]
> Set roaring war. To the dread rattling thunder
> Have I given fire, and rifted[14] Jove's stout oak
> With his own bolt. The strong-based promontory
> Have I made shake, and by the spurs[15] plucked up
> The pine and cedar. Graves at my command
> Have waked their sleepers, oped, and let 'em forth
> By my so potent art. But this rough magic
> I here abjure, and when I have required
> Some heavenly music—which even now I do—
> To work mine end upon their senses, that
> This airy charm is for, I'll break my staff,
> Bury it certain fathoms in the earth,
> And deeper than did ever plummet sound
> I'll drown my book.[16]   (act 5, scene 1)

Beyond this the English language cannot reach.

The changes in Shakespeare's style can be felt, but they cannot be exactly or scientifically analyzed, though there was at one time a fashion for reducing Shakespeare's verse to statistics and tables. These figures are of little value except as showing—what is obvious to any sensitive reader—that as Shakespeare developed, his verse was less restrained by metrical rules. But the judgment of style comes late, and only after much reading and experience—and there are no short cuts to the development of taste.

---

5. All of the plays written during the Overflowing Period are tragedies.   6. without leaving a footprint   7. the outgoing tide   8. tiny creatures, half the size of a puppet   9. unacceptable   10. fairy rings   11. fast growing, thought to be the work of fairies   12. rung at 9 P.M. warning people to go indoors   13. blue sky   14. split   15. roots   16. i.e., of magic spells

Shakespeare's Comedies Show Women as Equal Partners with Men

Germaine Greer

Germaine Greer asserts that marriage lies at the core of the social structure in Shakespeare's comedies. According to Greer, Shakespeare views marriage as a partnership between equals, sexually vibrant, committed, constant, and practical. Though Shakespeare never defines marriage directly through the voice of any of his characters, Greer says that an audience actively involved with the plays absorbs the definition. Greer cites a variety of examples in which this perception of marriage is apparent: *The Taming of the Shrew*, for instance, portrays two strong people working out a practical partnership. In other examples, Greer shows that women tend to honor commitments more readily than men, but that constant marriages offer the most satisfaction. Germaine Greer has been a lecturer in English literature at the University of Warwick. She is the author of *Sex and Destiny* and the best-selling *The Female Eunuch*.

In the comedies, [Shakespeare] came as close to exposition of a system of practical values as he could, without creating characters to serve as mouthpieces for his own ideas. Those values were derived from the culture of his Warwickshire ilk and diverged significantly from the received ideas of both city and court. At the core of a coherent social structure as he viewed it lay marriage, which for Shakespeare is no mere comic convention but a crucial and complex ideal. He rejected the stereotype of the passive, sexless, unresponsive female and its inevitable concomitant, the misogynist[1] con-

1. characterized by hatred of women

From Germaine Greer, *Shakespeare.* Copyright ©1986 by Germaine Greer. Reprinted by permission of Oxford University Press.

viction that all women were whores at heart. Instead he created a series of female characters who were both passionate and pure, who gave their hearts spontaneously into the keeping of the men they loved and remained true to the bargain in the face of tremendous odds. The women's steadfastness is in direct relation to their aggressiveness; the only Shakespearian woman to swerve from her commitment is Cressida, the passive manipulator of male desire and dissimulator of her own.

In rural households marriage was a partnership, involving hard physical labour on the part of the wife, as well as mutual forbearance in the long series of tribulations and reverses which country households had to survive.

> When all aloud the wind doth blow,
>   And coughing drowns the parson's saw,
> And birds sit brooding in the snow,
>   And Marian's nose looks red and raw,
> When roasted crabs hiss in the bowl,
> Then nightly sings the staring owl,
>   Tu-whit;
> Tu-who, a merry note,
> While greasy Joan doth keel the pot.

There can be no starker contrast to the ornate dalliance of the young lords in *Love's Labour's Lost* than the rustic song that replaces it on the stage (act 5, scene 2), described by an unnamed commentator as the harsh words of Mercury in place of the songs of Apollo. The inference is clear: love-making is easy when the fields are full of flowers and the girls sweet-smelling in freshly bleached linens, but marriages are made when the owl, Minerva's bird, makes its melancholy call from the dark fields and all must huddle round the smoky fire. The winter of the year is also a figure of the winter of human life, when love has to ripen into friendship and tolerance, regardless of the unsightliness of Marian's chapped face and Joan's ropy hair. . . .

PETRUCHIO'S SEARCH FOR A COMPETENT WIFE

The Taming of the Shrew is not a knockabout farce of wife-battering, but the cunning adaptation of a folk-motif to show the forging of a partnership between equals. Petruchio is not looking to fall in love, but to find a wife. His choice is based on self-interest in that he must find a woman who has some property of her own and who can help to run the estate he has just inherited. He chooses Kate as he would a horse, for her high mettle, and he must use at least as much intelligence and energy in bringing her to trust him, and to accept the bargain he offers, as he would in breaking a horse. . . .

Nowadays we have largely accepted the ideal of marriage which chooses a Beatrice for a Benedick, but the notion of egalitarian marriage was far from universal in Shakespeare's day, especially among the literate classes. In his early comedies he went to uncharacteristic lengths to provide clear exempla of the kind of relationship he saw as producing an appropriate outcome for a comedy. . . .

THE VIRTUE OF CONSTANT LOVE

The theme [of female fidelity] is mainly demonstrated as a constant male preoccupation, for Frank Ford in *The Merry Wives of Windsor*, Claudio in *Much Ado*, Posthumus in *Cymbeline*, *Othello*, and Leontes in *The Winter's Tale* all err in not trusting their wives. While female characters, having spontaneously and often suddenly committed themselves to a man, never swerve from the commitment, though in respecting it they may be called upon to risk their lives, Shakespeare's male characters, among them Proteus, Valentine, Orsino, Romeo, and Angelo, will break vows and transfer their affections in no longer than it takes to tell. Shakespeare seems to agree with Hermia in *A Midsummer Night's Dream* that men have broken more vows than women have ever spoken (act 1, scene 1). The inconstancy of men causes no great upheaval in the Shakespeare world, but when the solidity and truth of women are undermined, as in *Titus Andronicus*, *Troilus and Cressida*, and *King Lear*, the world regresses to savagery.

Shakespeare did not think of constancy as a psychosexual characteristic allied to masochism, but rather as an earthly manifestation of divine love, which is beyond gender. The turtledove in 'The Phoenix and the Turtle' is both a figure of constancy and male. The persona of the Sonnets cannot escape from his love vassalage, regardless of his beloved's perfidy, despite separation, calumny, public humiliation, and even the beloved's promiscuity and withdrawal of affection. Although he may permit himself ironies and denigrations, Shakespeare's persona continues to project the ideal of diamond-hard constancy, beyond death and dishonour, in despite of all treachery. . . .

The Abbess of *The Comedy of Errors* has waited out her

thirty-three-year separation in perfect celibacy. Shakespeare places a high value upon chastity, but he does not go so far as some of his contemporaries who thought that virtuous women had no physical desires. His witty ladies swap bawdy *doubles entendres*² with each other and with men, without sacrificing any of their own integrity. . . .

CRITICISM OF FALSE LOVE POETRY

In England in the 1590s poetical lovemaking seems to have become a kind of epidemic. Young men stuffed with 'taffeta phrases, silken terms precise' used them to turn the heads of silly women, disrupting the orderly progress of their courtship by humbler swains. Twice Elizabeth enacted severe penalties for the stealing of heiresses by the kinds of means deplored by Egeus in *Midsummer Night's Dream:*

> Thou, thou, Lysander, thou hast given her rhymes,
> And interchang'd love-tokens with my child:
> Thou hast by moonlight at her window sung
> With faining voice verses of feigning love,
> And stol'n the impression of her fantasy
> With bracelets of thy hair, rings, gauds, conceits,
> Knacks, trifles, nosegays, sweetmeats (messengers
> Of strong prevailment in unharden'd youth):
> With cunning hast thou filch'd my daughter's heart.
> (act 1, scene 1)

Moth, the wise little page in *Love's Labour's Lost*, utters a swingeing³ condemnation of love à la mode:

> . . . to jig off a tune at the tongue's end, canary to it with your feet, humour it with turning up your eyelids, sigh a note and sing a note, sometime through the throat as if you swallowed love with singing love, sometime through the nose as if you snuffed up love by smelling love; with your hat penthouse-like o'er the shop of your eyes; with your arms crossed on your thin-belly doublet like a rabbit on a spit; or your hands in your pocket like a man after the old painting; and keep not too long in one tune, but a snip and away. These are complements, these are humours, these betray nice wenches, that would be betrayed without these; and make them men of note (do you note, men?) that most are affected to these.
> (act 3, scene 1)

Moth implies that the affectations of such lovers as he describes are only likely to be effective with women who are easy or, in Elizabethan parlance, 'light'. Armado succeeds in seducing Jaquenetta, to be sure, but Jaquenetta is a silly

2. words or phrases with double meanings   3. scathing

country girl who has no defence against him. The young
lords accost the ladies of France with more evolved versions
of the same convention, but the ladies treat the whole business as a game, and a rather narcissistic and misconceived
game at that. None of Shakespeare's comic heroines is won
in a love game of this kind. Sylvia, Portia, and Olivia pre-
empt courtship by generously committing themselves. Ros-
alind/Ganymede and Viola/Cesario earn love by concealing
their femininity and thereby escaping the courtship process.
In this genderless (but not sexless) guise, they can express
their own versions of Moth's contempt. As Ganymede Rosalind can put a stop to Orlando's conventional pursuit,
which mainly consists in disfiguring trees with bad poetry,
not merely by mocking the stereotype of love melancholy
but by enacting a marriage ceremony before the courtship is
well under way. . . .

COUPLES DISPLAY VIBRANT, ENERGETIC ATTRACTION

For Shakespeare marriage was not simply a cliché for ending the action, although it became so in his lifetime. He was
profoundly interested in the paradox of creating a durable
social institution out of the volatile material of lovers' fantasies. In *Midsummer Night's Dream*, the lovers' broil is first
complicated and then sorted out by fairy magic, which
merges into ritual, which alone can reconcile Diana, goddess of chastity and childbirth, and Venus, the equally indis-
pensable avatar of sexual attraction, who have been poised
against each other in equal combat throughout the play. . . .

Oceans of ink were spilt in England during the turmoil of
the Reformation over the status of the married life, the rights
of lovers, and the interest of parents in their children's matings. The consensus was that parents did indeed have some
say in how their children disposed of themselves, but no par-
ent could force a child to marry against its will or refuse a
match which was otherwise suitable. In such cases the children could have redress to the ecclesiastical authorities. The
common people were scandalized by the dynastic marriages
arranged by the nobility who disposed of their children, according to the religious polemicists, as if they had been so
many cattle and sheep, especially when so many of the marriages clapped up with wards of the Crown later came to violent or adulterous ends. In treating the issue so seriously,
Shakespeare was giving form to the Protestant ideology of

marriage. . . .

We have become so used to marriage as a central theme for serious literature that it is not easy for us to estimate Shakespeare's originality in developing the idea of the complementary couple as the linchpin of the social structure. The medieval church regarded marriage as a second-rate condition, inferior both to virginity and celibacy, and to widowhood. Fraternal association was stressed at the expense of heterosexual commitment and intimacy, and one-sex hierarchy remained the pattern of social institutions. Shakespeare was writing after generations of religious upheaval in the course of which the hierarchical religious establishment had had to face a determined onslaught from champions of a more populist religion which drew very different lessons from the scriptures and demanded the right to follow the dictates of individual conscience.

Constant Love Defined
In Sonnet 116, Shakespeare defines his idea of constant love.

Let me not to the marriage of true minds
Admit impediments. Love is not love
Which alters when it alteration finds,
Or bends with the remover to remove.[1]
Oh no! It is an ever-fixèd mark   5
That looks on tempests and is never shaken.
It is the star to every wandering bark,
Whose worth's unknown, although his height be taken.
Love's not Time's fool,[2] though rosy lips and cheeks
Within his bending sickle's compass come.   10
Love alters not with his brief hours and weeks,
But bears it out even to the edge of doom.[3]
    If this be error and upon me proved,
    I never writ, nor no man ever loved.

1. wishes to change when the loved one is inconstant   2. mocked by time
3. doomsday

However they might differ on other issues, all the reformers vigorously defended the honourable estate of matrimony. In developing the character of Portia in *The Merchant of Venice*, for instance, Shakespeare used an existent motif, but his invention of the casket plot, so finely poised on the question of fathers' rights and heiresses' vulnerability, takes us through the whole development of a marriage relationship in a way that is profoundly original—it is because it has been so influential that it has come to seem to us utterly conventional.

The growth and development of the printing industry both stimulated and fed the desire for literacy. As literacy spread from above, social ideals seeped into literature from below. Straddling both written and verbal forms as a writer for the theatre, Shakespeare took up the cudgels on the side of the reformers, giving charm and life to their sometimes strident convictions. He projected the ideal of the monogamous heterosexual couple so luminously in his matings that they irradiate our notions of compatibility and co-operation between spouses to this day. . . .

Shakespeare imposed no exclusive criteria upon his vocabulary and erected no shibboleth[4] of purity of diction, such as was to hamstring Continental theatre for centuries. Dialect and jargon words were all grist to his voracious mill, laying the ground for an unrivalled linguistic heritage. His attitude was profoundly pragmatic; he took what was there, without troubling to consider whether it should have been there or not. . . .

SHAKESPEARE'S PRINCIPLE IS DEMOCRATIC

As long as Shakespeare remains central to English cultural life, it will retain the values which make it unique in the world, namely tolerance, pluralism, the talent for viable compromise, and a profound commitment to that most wasteful form of social organization, democracy. To an outsider such lack of system may seem amorphous, disorganized, and even hypocritical; from within it is evident that such an inclusive mode can be no more inconsistent than life itself. The puzzle is to discover the intrinsic ordering principle in apparent disorder. Perhaps the reason the principle eludes so many is that they are searching in the wrong place; in the theatre the beholder is the medium. The missing middle term in the Shakespearian proposition is our response. Without that there is and can be no argument.

4. language identifying a particular group or class

Strong Women Prevail in Shakespeare's Comedies

Angela Pitt

Angela Pitt argues that while men dominate Shakespeare's tragedies, women have the most prominent place in his comedies. All of the women characters in the comedies comply with the conventions of women's place in Elizabethan society as agents of happiness and order. Since comedies address social issues and resolve them happily, their purpose coincides with conventional roles for Elizabethan women. According to Pitt, the comedies contain a wide variety of strong women characters, ranging from a goat-girl to a queen. This variety permits contrasts and comparisons. For example, in *The Taming of the Shrew*, Katharina and Bianca have opposite personalities; in *As You Like It*, Rosalind and Celia reflect similar qualities in each other. Shakespearean scholar Angela Pitt was one of the first to research and publish information exclusively about Shakespeare's women. She has worked extensively at the Shakespeare Center Library in Stratford-on-Avon, England, and the Bodleian Library in Oxford, England.

If the dark realm of Shakespeare's tragedies is essentially men's territory, pride of place in the bright panorama of his comedies must surely belong to the women. Set alongside vivacious heroines . . . their male counterparts pale into insignificance. The character of Beatrice, indeed, has such force and charm that interest in her eventually takes over the play, despite the fact that her fate is not an important aspect of the original plot.

Why should the women leap into prominence? One reason may be that Shakespeare found their traditional attrib-

From Angela Pitt, *Shakespeare's Women* (Devon, UK: David & Charles, 1981). Reprinted by permission of the publisher.

utes of modesty, intuition and high-spiritedness highly suitable material for his comedies, and in varying blends and degrees, all his comic heroines have these characteristics. They never go beyond the bounds of what an Elizabethan audience would have found acceptable in a woman: it is rather that Shakespeare exalts the positive, rather than the negative traits. Any women that go against prevailing conventions are redeemed by the end of the play. Thus Katharina in *The Taming of the Shrew* is forced to give in to Petruchio's will, and Helena's unfeminine pursuit of Bertram is justified by the fact that he had failed to recognise her true worth; once he does so, she is submissive.

PRACTICAL AND KEEN-SIGHTED WOMEN

In Shakespeare, *Walter Raleigh describes Shakespeare's women characters as practical, no-nonsense people whose clear thinking cuts directly through men's self-deception.*

It is possible to extract from the plays some kind of general statement which, if it be not universally true of women, is at least true of Shakespeare's women. They are almost all practical, impatient of mere words, clear-sighted as to ends and means. They do not accept the premises to deny the conclusion, or decorate the inevitable with imaginative lendings. . . . The same quickness of apprehension is seen in those many passages where Shakespeare's women express their contempt for all the plausible embroidery of argument.

Another reason is that Shakespeare tacitly accepts the medieval idea of a hierarchy of nature in which woman is second to man. This means that the high seriousness of tragedy, with its intense focus on the fate of the individual, is an unsatisfactory setting for all but a very few women, and even these have their destinies inescapably intertwined with those of the tragic heroes. Comedy, on the other hand, allows for a broader, more detached view of society and a lighter tone. Although moral issues are not excluded (*The Merchant of Venice* is very much concerned with the contrast between material and spiritual wealth, as well as the nature of justice), we do not become anxious or painfully involved with the characters and, as the play progresses, hints are given that everything will turn out all right in the end. The characters themselves are frequently capricious, willing to compromise, and although they may well have faults, these do not inspire *fear* in the audience, as would be the case in tragedy. The plots too are full of twists and turns, surprises and coincidences. Until the final scene makes everything clear, no decision is incapable of being changed or reversed.

SHAKESPEARE'S COMEDIES HAVE HAPPY RESOLUTIONS

The forces of charm and whimsy are so strong in his comedies as to offer a further strong indication as to why Shakespeare favoured women characters for the leading roles. His choice was not a foregone conclusion, for other Elizabethan writers of comedy—notably Ben Jonson—let men dominate the stage as in tragedy. In the sixteenth century there were two traditions of dramatic comedy. One was the satirical revelation of human errors, played out so that the audience laughed to see their own follies so skilfully exposed. The other was to use as a setting some upset, sadness or problem that is subsequently resolved happily. Jonson wrote in the first, more hard-hitting tradition, where we laugh *at* the characters; Shakespeare in the second where we laugh *with* them. The hallmark of Shakespeare's comedies is consequently the move towards reconciliation and a restoration of order by the correct understanding of the original problem. Unlike the tragedies, which insist that chaos can be averted only by the elimination of those swept up in the catastrophe, the comedies show that problems can be solved and sorrows overcome if the situation is properly understood by those involved in it. Although we laugh at comedy, its purpose is as realistic and serious as that of tragedy: comedy shows us that happiness results from being able to face problems and put them into a balanced perspective; tragedy shows that misery and death result when dilemmas loom so large as to blot out all other aspects of life. As with the tragedies it is impossible to impose a strict formula on the construction of the comedies beyond the pattern mentioned above: that they all begin with the characters perplexed or threatened, but end happily. This general definition serves to embrace the eleven usually termed 'comedies' by editors and the five 'last plays'.

The agents of happiness and order in Shakespeare's comedies are the heroines, and their function is therefore of supreme importance. Not only do the women have the leading roles but also they are more numerous than in the other types of plays. They cover a wide range of types and classes:

a queen, a countess, princesses, dukes' daughters, a doctor's daughter, merchants' daughters, ladies-in-waiting, servants, shepherdesses, a goat-girl, nuns and prostitutes. This rich variety gives tremendous scope for contrasts and comparisons among the women themselves, as well as between men and women. With the exception of *The Tempest*, in which Miranda is the only woman, the other comedies present women as foils to each other. At its best, use of this device not only results in the idiosyncrasies of speech and behaviour, which make the heroines so very alive and credible, but also allows Shakespeare to reveal many subtle facets of their natures. . . .

TWO WOMEN AS OPPOSITES

'Fiery' would certainly apply to the temperament of Katharina in *The Taming of the Shrew*. Her taming, and particularly her last speech where she effectively shakes off her old personality to become her husband's slave, have excited strong reactions from modern audiences and critics. George Bernard Shaw was moved to write:

> . . . the last scene is altogether disgusting to modern sensibility. No man with any decency of feeling can sit it out in the company of a woman without being extremely ashamed of the lord-of-creation moral implied in the wager and the speech put into the woman's own mouth.

> (*Saturday Review*, 6 November 1897)

Shaw felt Petruchio's treatment of Katharina was a repugnant and progressive demoralisation of what had been a high-spirited young woman. To see if there is a basis for Shaw's criticism we need to look closely at the kind of characterisation meted out to the 'intolerable curst and shrewd and froward' heroine. . . .

In terms of the plot, her interests are secondary to those of her painfully insipid younger sister Bianca (who cannot get married until Katharina has found a husband), and at first there is the sense that despite her bravado she is merely a pawn. One of the few moments of true characterisation comes when Katharina, seeing Bianca's interests favoured above her own, exclaims with pain and passion to her father:

> Nay, now I see
> She is your treasure, she must have a husband;
> I must dance barefoot on her wedding-day,
> And, for your love to her, lead apes in hell.
> Talk not to me: I will go sit and weep. (act 2, scene 1)

Such personal revelations are rare. Katharina is never allowed a soliloquy and so we cannot learn her innermost thoughts. It is true that her character does change radically during the course of the play, but we observe it externally, through the comments of other characters and as a *fait accompli*[1] in Katharina herself. She exhibits the stereotyped characteristics of the 'shrewish' woman: violent behaviour, coarse language and a total disregard of authority. We are delighted by her vivid, energetic speech and her audacity when she threatens Hortensio, who has cracked jokes at her expense, that she would like 'to comb your noddle with a three legg'd stool' (act 1, scene 1), or when she bandies vulgarities with Petruchio:

PETRUCHIO.   Who knows not where a wasp does wear his
             sting? In his tail.

KATHARINA.   In his tongue.

PET.   Whose tongue?

KATH.   Yours, if you talk of tails; and so farewell.

PET.   What! With my tongue in your tail? Nay; come
             again. Good Kate, I am a gentleman.

KATH.   That I'll try. [*Striking him*]   (act 2, scene 1)

This is not to say that we can comprehend or sympathise with her character; we are simply knocked over by the anarchic power she unleashes. As Petruchio steadily and triumphantly out-shrews the shrew, this force abates in her until she has been cowed into total submissiveness. By the end of the play she does exemplify the sixteenth-century ideal of an adoring, concurring wife, but the very stereotyping of the two extremes of her behaviour suggests that Shakespeare may not have intended us to take her case altogether seriously. There is a pleasant irony, also, in that the faultless Bianca exhibits alarmingly shrewish tendencies in the final scene. She and Katharina effectively change places, for the infamous 'lord-of-creation' speech censured by Shaw, is in part directed at her. Perhaps Shakespeare is suggesting that there is a hint of shrewishness in all women. . . .

TWO WOMEN AS REFLECTIONS

From the outset[2] the close bond between Celia and Rosalind is emphasised. Rosalind's father has been banished by Duke

1. an irreversible action   2. of *As You Like It*

Frederick who has allowed her to stay in his court as company for his daughter Celia. To comfort Rosalind, Celia promises to return the wealth and land that have been taken from her father, as soon as Duke Frederick dies: 'and when I break that oath, let me turn monster. Therefore, my sweet Rose, my dear Rose, be merry.' Her motives spring entirely from her warm nature. When her father banishes Rosalind because he fears her popularity with his subjects, Celia speaks of the long time they have known each other. At first:

> I was too young that time to value her;
> But now I know her: if she be a traitor,
> Why so am I; we still have slept together,[3]
> Rose at an instant, learn'd, play'd, eat together;
> And whereso'er we went, like Juno's swans,
> Still we went coupled and inseparable.   (act 1, scene 3)

Such dedicated loyalty between women is not found elsewhere in Shakespeare, except between mistress and servant, where it cannot be equally balanced. Celia and Rosalind are 'coupled and inseparable'. Celia is willing to defy her father in order to support her friend, and when Rosalind cannot believe that Celia will leave with her, her friend gently rebukes her:

> Rosalind lacks then the love
> Which teacheth thee that thou and I am one:
> Shall we be sunder'd? shall we part, sweet girl?
> No: let my father seek another heir.   (act 1, scene 3)

DISGUISE MAKES ROSALIND STRONG

At this stage Celia is shown as the leader, the one who makes plans and acts on decisions. She supports Rosalind, who frequently needs comforting. There is a subtle change as soon as Rosalind adopts her disguise as a boy, for as she says:

> in my heart
> Lie there what hidden woman's fear there will
> We'll have a swashing and a martial outside. (act 1, scene 3)

Her outward appearance as a man gives her both confidence and courage. When she and Celia come to the Forest of Arden, she is the comforter when they are tired and a little frightened, for she adopts the man's role: 'doublet and hose ought to show itself courageous to petticoat.' Similarly, she is

---

3. *slept together*: not in a sexual sense. Although jokes about, and references to, homosexuality between men are to be found in Shakespeare, there is no equivalent for women. Celia is here referring to the Elizabethan habit of allowing members of the same sex to share the same bed.

now the one who makes arrangements for their new life-style in the Forest, by buying a cottage and a flock of sheep. Although there is no suggestion that affection between them diminishes, from this point Rosalind commands more of the audience's attention than Celia, and she is shown as more resourceful and robust than her friend.

Partly this is because of the plot. When they arrive in the Forest, Rosalind is already in love with Orlando, now banished like her, but Celia has no one. It is, incidentally, further proof of Celia's selfless loyalty that there is not an ounce of jealousy in her. She professes to love Orlando for her friend's sake and apart from teasing her a little when Rosalind is desperate for news of him, does everything she can to bring them together. She does not play gooseberry for long, however, because she falls in love with Oliver, the once-wicked but now reformed elder brother of Orlando. Their courtship is non-existent from the audience's point of view, but we are told within two scenes of their meeting that: 'They are in the very wrath of love, and they will together: clubs cannot part them.' Celia's destiny is rapidly worked out in this way because by Act V the interest is firmly centred on Rosalind, whose disguise has provoked a number of curious situations.

ROSALIND'S DECEPTION-WITHIN-A-DECEPTION

Like Julia in *The Two Gentlemen of Verona*, her wearing of boy's clothes has enabled her to get close to her lover and find out the truth of his feelings for her. Rosalind does not become his page, but proposes a more complicated relationship, which involves a deception-within-a-deception.

What she suggests is that Orlando 'cures' himself of his love by coming to her cottage every day to woo her, giving her the name of Rosalind. The situation that emerges is fraught with irony and ambiguity: Rosalind, assuming the personality of a youth, Ganymede, is wooed by her real lover, who calls her Rosalind while believing she is a boy! The choice of the name Ganymede[4] provides a homosexual joke to add to the general confusion of identities, and an additionally discordant element is added when a shepherdess, Phebe, falls in love with the disguised Rosalind. The plot is as swift-moving as a situational comedy like *The Comedy of*

---

4. youthful lover of Zeus, as well as being his cup-bearer

Errors, but the tone is lighter, funnier and, apart from being assured of a happy ending, we are unable to predict what will happen from moment to moment. It is also one of Shakespeare's more ambitious plots: the parallel loves of Celia and Oliver, Rosalind and Orlando, are contrasted not only with that of the idealised pastoral figures of Phebe and Silvius, but also the amorous cavortings of the sluttish goat-girl Audrey and the court jester Touchstone.

When Rosalind puts on her woman's clothes once more she retains the independent spirit she assumed in disguise, for she is the voice of order prevailing over chaos. By the end of Act V she is the only character with the knowledge necessary to unravel all the tangled relationships that bewilder her companions and she dominates the final scene in the play, pairing off all the couples, including herself and Orlando. From being a fearful refugee in the Forest of Arden, she has changed into a self-possessed young woman whose opinions are sought and respected. The light-heartedness, wit and intelligence are still there, but she has become more thoughtfully aware of others than before. Her character-development far outstrips her cousin's, for Celia remains essentially the same after her arrival in the forest. There is no doubt that Rosalind's sudden maturity is initiated by her role-playing as a boy, for she has the chance of a type of freedom and command that is denied to Celia....

THE GAME OF LOVE

The game of love is present in all the comedies and last plays. Sometimes it is almost hidden, as in *Cymbeline*, where one player wrongly accuses another of breaking the rules and there are many terrible moments before the game can be resumed. Occasionally people play it without even realising that they have begun to make the moves, like Beatrice in *Much Ado*. Most often there are two or three different games going on at the same time, but the players, for a gamut of reasons, are unable to settle into balanced partnerships until the end. In some measure each of these love-games is a game of chess, the symbol suggested for Miranda and Ferdinand.[5] We cannot help but notice that Shakespeare is paying an indirect tribute to the importance of women, for in chess the most versatile, powerful and treasured piece is the queen.

5. in *The Tempest*

Shakespeare's Comedies Combine Convention and Personal Style

George Gordon

In an Oxford lecture, George Gordon argues that none of the established theories of comedy define Shakespeare's comedies. According to Gordon, they do not follow Elizabethan prescriptions in that Shakespeare is too poetic and too romantic, his satire is too good-natured, and his women are too prominent. Yet, Gordon argues, Shakespeare employs all of the traditional theatrical conventions. He uses the usual stage tricks, such as disguises. He uses stock characters. He uses the traditional love plots of boy gets girl with happy endings. But, asserts Gordon, Shakespeare makes the conventions his own and gives a warm humanity to each of his comedies. George Gordon began teaching English at Magdalen College, Oxford, in 1907. He was professor of English literature at Leeds, Merton College, Oxford, and Trinity College, Cambridge, and he lectured in Norway and Sweden and at the Royal Institution in England.

Shakcspeare is too poetic for Comedy proper. Comedy deals with familiar surroundings and with society as it exists; but Shakespeare the romantic habitually does neither. There is, of course, much truth in this. Recall that romantic world in which Shakespeare is happiest—the world of his comedies and young people—that incomparable rainbow mixture of Old England and Utopia—and you will observe that most of these plays begin with some artificial seclusion or segregation from the world. The curtain goes up; and at once, or in a scene or two, the door is shut on ordinary life. Except in *The Comedy of Errors* and *The Merchant of Venice*, where the

From George Gordon, *Shakespearian Comedy and Other Studies*. Reprinted by permission of Oxford University Press.

play opens on a public mart, hardly anybody goes to business in these Shakespearian latitudes, or seems to be obliged to get up at any particular time—though, on the whole, except for the drinkers, all Shakespeare's people like the morning. The scene being staged for Love, it is essential that its young people should be idle, should have time on their hands. No enemy of Love like work! Everyone of importance lives on his or her estate; or in Arcadia[1]—where there are no clocks, and everybody helps everybody else. It is a world of delicious make-believe....

COMIC CHARACTERS OF THE WOODS AND WILDS

In Comedy, *English novelist George Meredith praises Shakespeare's comic characters, who live in an enlarged world of poetic imagination.*

Shakespeare is a well-spring of characters which are saturated with the comic spirit; with more of what we will call blood-life than is to be found anywhere out of Shakespeare; and they are of this world, but they are of the world enlarged to our embrace by imagination, and by great poetic imagination. They are, as it were—I put it to suit my present comparison—creatures of the woods and wilds, not in walled towns, not grouped and toned to pursue a comic exhibition of the narrower world of society. Jaques, Falstaff and his regiment, the varied troop of clowns, Malvolio, Sir Hugh Evans and Fluellen (marvelous Welshmen!), Benedick and Beatrice, Dogberry, and the rest, are subjects of a special study in the poetically comic.

I know nothing more artistically interesting or more truly Elizabethan than to see Shakespeare at work on this fiction of segregation—on this deliciousness of Nowhere; to see him set it up in the pride of fancy, and undermine it with the pride of life. For in Shakespeare—however fantastic and Utopian the fiction may be—Life always comes in and claims its due. Partly, as I said, this is good Elizabethan, for there never was a more Utopian or a more practical age. It is their peculiar mixture, their elixir: and perhaps it is the secret of every great age. Partly it is the healthy conscience of Shakespeare, of a man who all his life, headache or no headache, had to work for his living—and to maintain, among all his

1. an isolated pastoral place

dreams and fancies, a steady balance with reality. Shakespeare was never permitted, like so many of our later poets, to practise the art of segregation in his own life. . . .

SHAKESPEARE'S GOOD-NATURED SATIRE

Shakespeare, then, poetic as he is, does not neglect the work of Comedy. But it is said that he is too good-natured, too kind for Comedy. Comedy has a mission, and in the interests of society must have the courage to be cruel, to use the lash. In the art of cruelty, and in whipcracking generally, it must be admitted that Shakespeare is defective. Not that he is without satire: he makes fun, of course, like all comedians, of the follies of his time. . . .

If his characters are corrected, the correction seems not to come from some external power: they seem to do it for one another. If exposures are made, it is still a family affair. Shakespeare's comedies, regarded purely as Comedy, present us with a holy war, conducted without malice or bloodshed on Egotism, Sentimentalism, Pedantry, and Self-importance: on precisely those weaknesses and follies, in short, which, without being criminal, make bad citizens and bad neighbours— tiresome husbands and tiresome wives—which make men and women unsociable, and unfit for the friendly purposes of life. They say to Life, these people, like peevish children, that they 'won't play', and are laughed by Shakespearian Comedy into the game.

Let me take a slender but typical example from the class of Egotistic Lovers. It cannot have escaped you how very egotistic and unsocial lovers can be. They have a roughish time of it in Shakespeare's comedies, but all, let me remind you, within the family. We are privileged, in *Much Ado*, to see the first dawning of Claudio's passion for Hero; and *whom* should he confide in but Benedick his friend? It was a rash step. For it is a law of Shakespearian Comedy—part of its family code—that every excess of egotism or sentiment shall be treated as an illness; and first aid, not always of the gentlest, shall be instantly applied.

CLAUDIO. Benedick, didst thou note the daughter of Signior Leonato?

BENE. I noted her not; but I looked on her.

CLAUDIO. Is she not—a—modest young lady?

BENE. [*looking more closely at him*] Do you question me, as an honest man should do, for my simple true judgement; or would you have me speak after my custom, as being a professed tyrant to their sex?

CLAUDIO. No; I pray thee; speak in sober judgement.

BENE. Why, i' faith, methinks she's too low for a high praise, too brown for a fair praise, and too little for a great praise; only this commendation I can afford her, that were she other than she is, she were unhandsome, and being no other but as she is—I do not like her.

CLAUDIO. Thou thinkest I am in sport: I pray thee tell me truly how thou likest her.

BENE. Would you buy her, that you inquire after her?

CLAUDIO. Can the world buy such a jewel?

BENE. [*in the same tone*] Yea, and a case to put it into.

A little unkind, perhaps, but how *good* for Claudio! And the game is not one-sided. It is tit for tat. Claudio will have his chance at Benedick, when *he* goes the same reluctant way: and so, in Shakespeare's manner, every excess acts physician to every other. It is first aid all round.

SHAKESPEARE'S WOMEN DEFLATE CLEVER TALKERS

There are also—if I may take another example of this family treatment—there are also the *Verbalists*, the *Fine and Clever Talkers*, whose brains have gone to their heads. Shakespeare in private life, was, on unimpeachable evidence, a great talker himself, and there can have been nothing about this interesting weakness that he did not know. But Life, as he knew still better—as all women have always known— is not run by clever talk—is, on the contrary, often impeded by it. In the comedies of Shakespeare nearly all the principal offenders in this way are *men*: it was a weakness of the age; and it is noticeable that their punishment and their cure are generally placed by Shakespeare in the hands of women. I need recall only Biron in *Love's Labour's Lost* and Jaques in *As You Like It.*

Shakespeare's women, of course, can play this verbal game themselves, and do, in fact, as we know, play it admirably; but only, as a rule, sufficiently to protect themselves and keep the ball rolling: it is generally to be suspected that their hearts are not wholly in it. If they are interested in a man, it is very often not so much what he *says* that interests them, as what he does *not* say, and might perhaps have said. All Shakespeare's gentlewomen have a gift of silence; and, unprovoked, are naturally of few words.

> SHALLOW. Here comes fair Mistress Anne. Would I were young for your sake, Mistress Anne.
>
> ANNE. The dinner is on the table.

There is a striking passage in Cymbeline, where Imogen is forced by the importunity of Cloten to state her full mind about his proposals. She does so, and then—even to Cloten—apologizes for it, feeling it to be out of character:

> I am much sorry, sir,
> You put me to forget a lady's manners,
> By being so verbal.

It is, as you know, a jest of all time that *women* are the talkative sex; and all the jest books of Shakespeare's day were full of it. It shows the admirable perception of Shakespeare that he was not deceived. Whatever washerwomen may do, Shakespeare's *grandes dames*, his Elizabethan great ladies, unless provocation drives them, speak quietly and to the point....

SHAKESPEARE USED CONVENTIONS OF COMEDY

Shakespeare, above almost every other comic dramatist of his rank, used the theatrical stock-in-trade of his time, and in his earlier plays—since the rest of the cupboard is barer—the anatomy of these conventions is more easily seen. Take, for example, *The Two Gentlemen of Verona*. All the stage-tricks of the comic and romantic drama of western Europe, some of them hoary with antiquity, are to be found there: the window and balcony, the inevitable serenade, the rope-ladder, the convenient Friar, outlaws and a forest. Julia, the first of a long line of Shakespearian heroines in hose and doublet, timidly starts a practise which is followed with more confidence by Viola, Rosalind, and Imogen, and in *The Merchant of Venice* not by one woman, but by all—a raid on the masculine wardrobe. Here also is to be met the first of those inimitable servingmen, half-valets, half-clowns, without whom no Shakespearian comedy is to be complete: Launce[2] has many collaterals[3] in the works of Shakespeare, each richer and more mouldy than the last: and when I say mouldy, I use it in an honourable sense, as of a cheese.

None of the stock characters and devices are peculiar to

2. the clown in *Merchant of Venice* 3. parallels, similar types

Shakespeare, or his own invention. He uses the old business over and over again, never tiring of it, apparently, nor his audience either; and we think of it as Shakespearian because he did it so much better than anyone else, and with an art so constantly improving not only upon his contemporaries but upon himself. In the end it is steeped in poetry, and in *The Tempest* passes away in a pageant not of this world.

This conservatism of Shakespeare, this contentment with the convention, goes deeper still, and affects the very postulates of his plays. Every play that ever was written begins with a request. It asks us to admit something. Suppose, says the dramatist, these people to have come together, and to be in these positions, let me show you what happens. Accept this hypothesis, and everything follows. Refuse it, and the play cannot go on. I am describing the first rule of the game. Shakespeare, in his comedies, usually asks a good deal of us—puts a strain on our credulity. And this is one of his disabilities, according to the critics, for the social and corrective mission of *la haute comédie*,[4] or, as they call it, Comedy Proper.

SUSPENSION OF DISBELIEF

Take an unvarnished example. If you have read *The Comedy of Errors*, you are aware of the monstrous improbability on which that play is founded. The pair of twins so exactly alike that even their mother cannot tell them apart—so much we are prepared to accept: it is well known that this may happen: and any dramatist or story-teller is entitled to get all the fun he can out of their mistaken identities. But Shakespeare is not content with this.

> That very hour, and in the self-same inn,
> A meaner woman was delivered
> Of such a burden, male twins, both alike.

The father of the first pair, somewhat struck by the circumstance—he calls it 'strange', being a rich man—buys the second pair from their parents, who were very poor, and brings them up to be attendants on his sons. What more is wanted? They take ship to go home; along comes the obedient storm of the romancer; the ship founders; the family is dispersed; rich twin sticks to poor twin, each in his pair—the dramatist waves his hand—twenty years have passed; and the play, ladies and gentlemen, he announces, is about to

4. high comedy

begin. The question is, shall we, revolted by these demands on our credulity, refuse the invitation, decline to walk up?

On this I would remark that, though Shakespeare never again asks quite so much of us, he continues to ask a good deal. . . .

All lectures on Shakespeare's comedies tend to become lectures on Shakespeare's women, for in the comedies they have the front of the stage. Of most of Shakespeare's plays, as you are aware, no such feminine predominance can be asserted. It is absent from his English Histories, and from most of his Tragedies also. Whoever, when studying the Tragedies of Shakespeare, keeps his eyes sentimentally on the women—keeps thinking too much of Ophelia in *Hamlet* and of Cordelia in *King Lear*, of Lady Macbeth rather than of her husband, and of Desdemona rather than Othello—let us agree to thrust a slightly faded lily into that Shakespearian student's hand and push him gently out of doors.

PROMINENCE OF STRONG WOMEN

In the world of the comedies, on the other hand, he may gratify his bent to the utmost. For it is true of most of Shakespeare's comedies, as it is of daily life, that where the woman is, there also, probably, is the root and heart of the matter. Shakespeare was a great student of women, and his portraits of women have never been surpassed: women of all ranks and ages—from the queen to the dairymaid—and from fifty to fifteen. The best of artists have their limits; but in this bright particular region Shakespeare would appear to have had none. From Cleopatra to Miranda—which I take to be very nearly the full span—he is equally at home, and has the whole range of femininity at his command. . . .

When we turn to the comedies of Shakespeare, we enter another world: a world of which the first quality is—what? With the English histories in my mind—as they were in Shakespeare's—I should say that its first quality is that it is a world made safe for women: a climate in which a girl can be happy and come to flower, in which the masculine element drops its voice. Certainly, whatever may have happened on the historical scene, here, in this land of Arcady, in this Utopia of Romance, Man, mere Man, lays down his arms. There is never any question who rules in these latitudes: it is Woman, Woman, all the time. I suppose no man ever grudged these glittering heroines, these Rosalinds, Violas, and Portias, their overpowering success. They so evidently deserve to win, and to put man in his place; for no more charming, witty, rebellious—and, I would remind you, level-headed—young women ever danced across a stage. Shake-speare's pen seems to move with a new grace and vivacity the moment one of them enters. . . .

It is amusing to compare these young women of the come-dies with the young men who run after them; in other words, with their future husbands, for in Comedy, as you know, we all get our girls in the end. As the old play has it—'Jack hath Jill, And nought goes ill'. They are in love with each other, these young people—this couple and that couple; though the young women, as is only right and proper, are mostly rather slow to admit it. But mark, I would ask you, the difference in their behaviour! The young men are fine fellows, handsome, debonair, devoted; but it can hardly fail to have struck you how much better they are at talking than at doing anything! When any real business has to be done, when any difficult arrangement has to be made—who does it? Who makes it? Always the woman. The young men seem quite helpless, and while they are occupied in looking handsome and worthy of their parts, the women make the plans. . . .

What, then, to conclude, is the secret of Shakespeare's comedies: of their lasting beauty and power? It is no mystery. Their secret is the secret . . . of light and air. A brilliant sun-shine inundates and glorifies them. The spirit that inspires them is an absolute humanity unashamed and unafraid. You may sometimes be shocked by the language of your com-pany; you may be shocked, but you will never be cold-shoul-dered. You may sometimes be incommoded by the diversity of your experience: but you are never melancholy, and you are never outcast. The World, which is the foundation of sanity, is always with you or near you. The World is made of Life and Hope: the Shakespearian Comedy is a portrait of the World. Boccaccio has been called 'the escape from Dante'. What is Shakespeare the 'escape from'? Shall I be accused of professional cynicism if I suggest that he is possibly the es-cape from his critics? Some of our modern analysts think that Shakespeare, in his comedies, might have gone deeper. The direction of his comedies, as of Boccaccio's stories, is rather to width than depth: but what is wrong with width? 'The world *is* wide, and its width supplies a kind of profun-dity in another dimension.'

Imagery Establishes Atmosphere and Background in the Comedies

Caroline F.E. Spurgeon

Caroline F.E. Spurgeon, who has counted and classi-fied images in Shakespeare's plays, says that imagery gives atmosphere and background to the comedies. The imagery in *A Midsummer Night's Dream*, for ex-ample, gives the play a sense of woodland beauty and the presence of the moon and moonlight. The moon also measures time and movement. Nature images evoke a feeling of the seasons in the English countryside and the sound of birds in summer. Ac-cording to Spurgeon, the imagery of *Twelfth Night* reflects the play's mixture of music, romance, sad-ness, beauty, and wit. In *As You Like It*, the images amuse the audience with their wit. Spurgeon says that Rosalind's exchanges with Orlando are filled with similes and metaphors, as are the lines spoken by Jaques and Touchstone.

Like *A Midsummer Night's Dream*, this play has an out-door country atmosphere, created with images of animals, trees, weather, and objects used by country dwellers. *The Taming of the Shrew* has fewer poetic images; some are beautiful comparisons of Katherina with roses and a hazel twig, and others describe Petruchio's taming activities and his boisterous attitude toward his success. An expert on Shakespeare's imagery, Caroline F.E. Spurgeon was professor emerita of English literature at the University of London.

As far as there is any continuous symbolism in the imagery of the comedies, its function would seem to be to give at-

From Caroline F.E. Spurgeon, *Shakespeare's Imagery and What It Tells Us* (New York: Cambridge University Press, 1935). Reprinted by permission of Cambridge University Press.

mosphere and background, as well as to emphasise or re-echo certain qualities in the plays.

A MIDSUMMER NIGHT'S DREAM

Thus, in *A Midsummer Night's Dream*, we know that what we feel overpoweringly is the woodland beauty of the dreaming summer night, and it is only when we look closer that we realise in some measure how this sensation is brought about.

The influence and presence of the moon are felt throughout, largely through the imagery, from the opening lines when the noble lovers impatiently measure the days to their wedding by the waning of the old moon and the coming of the new,

> like to a silver bow
> New-bent in heaven,

to the end, when Puck tells us the 'wolf behowls the moon', and that it is therefore the time of night for the fairies' frolic.

Time and movement are both measured by her, for mortals as well as for Puck and the fairies; the lovers make their tryst for the moment on the morrow,

> when Phoebe doth behold
> Her silver visage in the watery glass;

the fairies compass the globe 'swifter than the wandering moon'. She is the 'governess of floods', and controls not only the weather, but also the fiery shafts of love which at will she quenches in her 'chaste beams'; she symbolises the barren air of the cloister, where the sisters live

> Chanting faint hymns to the cold fruitless moon;

she serves, as does the sun, for an emblem of steadfast constancy; and Hermia cries she would as soon believe a hole might be bored in the centre of the earth and the moon creep through it, as that Lysander should willingly have left her.

The word 'moon' occurs twenty-eight times, three and a half times more often than in any other play, partly of course owing to the prominence of moonshine, often addressed as 'moon', as a character in the comedy of the 'homespuns'. 'Moonlight' naturally also occurs unusually often: indeed Shakespeare only mentions moonlight in his plays eight times altogether, and six of these are in *A Midsummer Night's Dream*, as is also his only reference to moonbeams. His single use of 'starry' is also here, when Oberon tells Puck to cover the 'starry welkin', and the sensation of starlight, which is constant (the fairies dance by 'spangled starlight sheen', Puck accuses Demetrius of 'bragging to the stars', if moonshine be gone Thisbe will find her lover by starlight, and so on), is largely owing to the many comparisons to the stars which come naturally to those who are looking at them, as when Demetrius assures Hermia that though she has pierced his heart, and is a murderer, she looks

> as bright, as clear,
> As yonder Venus in her glimmering sphere,

and Lysander declares that Helena

> more engilds the night
> Than all yon fiery oes and eyes of light.

This moonlit background, then, partly supplies the dreaming and enchanted quality in the play, which is reinforced by woodland beauty. This is drawn largely from two sources, closely allied and sometimes melting into one: the high proportion of poetical images—ninety-five out of a total of a hundred and fourteen—considerably higher than in any other comedy, and the very large number of nature images, including animals and birds. These Shakespeare always has, but their number here is unusual, for in addition to those listed under 'nature', there are many which have to be classified under other headings, which really, all the time, are calling up country pictures before us. Thus the 'green corn' which

> Hath rotted ere his youth attain'd a beard,

which is really a personification, brings to the mind above all else the sight of the fields at the end of many a wet English summer, just as the description of the way

> the spring, the summer,
> The childing autumn, angry winter, change
> Their wonted liveries,

which comes under 'clothes', really presents us with a pageant of the swift succession of the seasons in their many-coloured garb.

Even the measurement of time is made, not only by the moon, but also by the cock-crow, the 'middle summer's spring', and the 'lightning in the collied[1] night', by the greening of the wheat and the coming of the hawthorn buds, by the mating of the birds and the swimming powers of the

---

1. dark, like coal

leviathan, by dawn and sunrise, by a shadow and a sound.

And the birds too, whose song and sound are heard throughout, as it should be in an English woodland play, the dove, the nightingale, the rook, and the lark—these are, as with Shakespeare always, used as a measure of all kinds of activities and sense-values: of light movement, 'hop as light as bird from brier', of sweet sound, 'more tuneable than lark to shepherd's ear', of colour-sense,

> high Taurus' snow,
> Fann'd with the eastern wind, turns to a crow
> When thou hold'st up thy hand,

or of headlong scattered flight, as when the wild geese or russet-pated choughs,[2]

> Rising and cawing at the gun's report,
> Sever themselves and madly sweep the sky.

Even in the farce of the rustics we get—as it were by chance—a splash of nature-beauty flung by the way such as:

> Of colour like the red rose on triumphant brier,

and in the play as a whole the succession of imaginative pictures crystallising experiences, emotions, and sensations familiar to all English nature lovers has never been surpassed by Shakespeare himself. These are all well known, for they are among our greatest poetry, and a score of them could be named in this play alone, but two must suffice here.

We English all know that delightful mid-season of early autumn when the night frosts nip the late summer flowers, and through which the hardy monthly roses persist in gaily blooming, but it is Shakespeare who has painted the poet's picture of it for ever, with its exquisite mingling of sharp air and sweet scents, in the Fairy Queen's description of what was probably the experience of many a gardener at the end of the cold wet summer of 1594:

> we see
> The seasons alter: hoary-headed frosts
> Fall in the fresh lap of the crimson rose;
> And on old Hiems'[3] thin and icy crown
> An odorous chaplet of sweet summer buds
> Is, as in mockery, set.

We have most of us seen a summer's sunrise over the sea, but Shakespeare has immortalised the pageant for us in a riot of colour and beauty when we watch with Oberon,

2. a crowlike bird with red legs   3. winter's

Even till the eastern gate, all fiery-red,
Opening on Neptune with fair blessed beams,
Turns into yellow gold his salt green streams.

No wonder Keats underscored this play in parts almost continuously, for sheer poetry, nature and moonlight were his loves, and he found them all here together to his hand, as nowhere else in literature, in rich and joyous abundance. And these, largely through the imagery we have been analysing, have stamped their special impress on the play, which leaves us, as it has left myriads, over nearly three and a half centuries, amazed and bewitched by beauty and the strange power of the poet's pen. . . .

TWELFTH NIGHT

In *Twelfth Night* the types of images reflect subtly and accurately the rather peculiar mixture of tones in the play, music, romance, sadness and beauty interwoven with wit, broad comedy, and quick-moving snapping dialogue.

The first thing one notices is that out of a hundred images there are only fourteen which can be called poetical, but these are either peculiarly beautiful, and very well known, such as the

sweet sound
That breathes upon a bank of violets
Stealing and giving odour!

(needing no emendation to my mind); Viola's description of how she let

concealment, like a worm i' the bud,
Feed on her damask cheek,

Olivia's purging 'the air of pestilence', and the 'babbling gossip of the air' crying out her name; or they are vivid and unforgettable, like Sir Andrew's hair which 'hangs like flax on a distaff',[4] and the duke's mind which is 'a very opal'; or inimitable pictures, such as Fabian's of Malvolio as a 'rare turkeycock' jetting 'under his advanced plumes'; or his threat to Sir Toby, that having sailed into the north of his lady's opinion he will hang there 'like an icicle on a Dutchman's beard'.

Further, one remarks that this play has, even for a comedy, an unusual number (sixteen) of 'topical' images, amusing, quaint, ingenious and witty, mostly in the prose parts

---

4. a staff that holds unspun flax or wool from which thread is drawn

and the Sir Toby scenes, such as his declaration that 'he's a coward . . . that will not drink to my niece, till his brains turn o' the toe like a parish-top',[5] or his direction to Sir Andrew to scout for him 'at the corner of the orchard like a bum-baily',[6] Viola's message that she will stand at Olivia's door 'like a sheriff's post', Maria's well-known comparison of the lines in Malvolio's face to the 'new map', the clown's comparison of a cheveril[7] glove to a good wit, or Sir Toby's sheet of paper 'big enough for the bed of Ware[8] in England'. These and many more give a lightness and brilliance to the play which must have delighted the early audiences, and which keep alive the atmosphere of repartee and topical fun which is one of the characteristics of this sophisticated and delicious comedy. . . .

As You Like It

As You Like It fairly scintillates with wit, largely in the form of images. Celia and Rosalind's dialogue is full of tropes, as in the opening of Act 1, scene 3, and the fun for the onlookers is to watch the two girls catching the jests dexterously from each other, tossing them to and fro like shuttlecocks.

Rosalind's gay, chaffing talk with Orlando is, similarly, a mass of verbal fireworks in metaphor and simile, sometimes a kind of 'set piece' to amuse the audience, like the comparison of time to an ambling, trotting or galloping nag, which covers some twenty-six lines, sometimes a quick bright shower of sparks, as in her retort, 'make the doors upon a woman's wit and it will out at the casement; shut that and 'twill out at the keyhole; stop that, 'twill fly with the smoke out at the chimney'.

Jaques is one of the great simile makers in Shakespeare, and his long and formal 'set piece' of the seven ages is probably the best known passage in the plays. Touchstone's wit, too, scintillates with simile, reminding us at times of Lyly,[9] by his delight in the mere sound of a succession of comparisons, as when he answers Jaques' query 'Will, you be married, motley?' with the euphuistic[10] refrain, 'As the ox hath his bow, sir, the horse his curb and the falcon her bells, so man hath his desires; and as pigeons bill, so wedlock would

5. a large spinning top used by villagers on frosty days when it was too cold to work   6. sheriff's officer who made arrests for debt   7. kidskin   8. a famous bed that could hold seven couples at a time; now in the Victoria and Albert Museum in London   9. John Lyly, who wrote *The Anatomy of Wit*   10. identifies a style of wit evolving from Lyly's *Euphues*

be nibbling'.[11] More often he is 'swift and sententious' with deep meaning behind his words; as when, whimsically intrigued with the blank incomprehension of Audrey, he plays to Jaques as audience, and, in the form of a simile, makes the oblique reference, easily recognised by his larger audience, to the death of Marlowe[12] by Ingram Frysar's dagger in the so-called quarrel over 'le recknynge' in Eleanor Bull's house at Deptford:

> When a man's verses cannot be understood, nor a man's good wit seconded with the forward child, understanding, it strikes a man more dead than a great reckoning in a little room.

The double allusion here, first to the facts of Marlowe's death, and secondly to his well-known line,

> Infinite riches in a little room,

makes the meaning of the reference a certainty, and is also entirely in keeping with Touchstone's subtle rapierlike wit.

This simile is perhaps the most interesting 'topical' allusion in the whole of Shakespeare, but the entire play is remarkable for an unusual number of what may be called 'topical' similes—similes, that is, which refer to things familiar to the Elizabethan audience, but not to us, or indeed in many cases to any but the people of that day. Such are Rosalind's threat that she will weep for nothing 'like Diana in the fountain', by which she may mean the fountain set up in Cheapside in 1596, described by Stowe, with the image of Diana with 'water prilling from her naked breast'; or Silvius' description of the common executioner asking pardon from his victim before chopping off his head; or Orlando's retort to Jaques' taunting query as to whether he has not culled his 'pretty answers' out of the posies on rings, 'Not so; but I answer you right painted cloth, from whence you have studied your questions', referring to the familiar painted canvas hangings for rooms, which often had the words spoken by the characters written in above them, or issuing from them in a balloon, as in eighteenth-century broadsides.

Sometimes these topical allusions throw a sinister light on current customs or characters, as in Rosalind's description of the dark house and the whip meted out to madmen, and Celia's comparison of the oath of a lover to the word of a tapster,[13] 'they are both the confirmer of false reckonings'.

---

11. getting at a man   12. Shakespeare's contemporary, Christopher   13. the potboy in a tavern who brings the drinks

All these topical similes seem to strike and re-echo the key and tune of the play, which, though set in the green-wood, where they 'fleet the time carelessly', is yet so clearly written to please a highly sophisticated town audience, which delights in bouts of sparkling wit 'made of Atalanta's[14] heels', is ever alive to double meanings, and is quick as lightning to seize on and laugh at a local or topical allusion.

Finally, as in *A Midsummer Night's Dream*, the number of nature images is very high. Of nature and animals together there are more in *As You Like It* than in any other comedy and these play their part in the general atmosphere. It has been pointed out, that although there is, in the play, a peculiarly vivid feeling of outdoor country life, there is very little nature description, indeed only two short passages, one of the sheepcote 'fenced about with olive trees', and one of the oak 'whose boughs were mossed with age'. But although there is little set description, there are, as in *Much Ado*, continual touches which keep ever before the audience the background of nature, such as the opening scene in the orchard, the duke's references to winter's wind and trees and running brooks, the stag hunt, the shepherd's cot, Amiens' song, Orlando's verses, the meal under the shade of melancholy boughs, Corin's shepherd's talk, the foresters and their song, and the exquisite 'foolish song' at the end, to which Touchstone counted it but time lost to listen.

But a still more subtle and less obvious way of intensifying the country and open air feeling is through simile and metaphor, and of this full use is made, such as the picture of walking through a thorny wood, in the girls' jests about briers and burs; the charming little glimpse, given by Silvius in his modesty, of gleaning the broken ears in the harvest field; or even so tiny a touch as Celia's description of finding Orlando 'under a tree, like a dropped acorn'.

We find an unusual number of animal similes, the highest in any of the comedies, and these add greatly to the life of the country pictures: the doe going to find her fawn to give it food, the weasel sucking eggs, chanticleer crowing, the wild goose flying, pigeons feeding, and such vivid glimpses of animal passion and emotion as those given us by Rosalind, 'there was never anything so sudden but the fight of two rams', 'I will be more jealous of thee than a Barbary

14. a swift runner, but led astray by cupidity

cock-pigeon over his hen'.

We are constantly reminded of Shakespeare's favourite haunts of garden and orchard in the many similes from grafting, pruning and weeding, as in Rosalind's chaff with Touchstone about 'graffing' with the medlar, Orlando's warning to Adam that in staying with him he prunes 'a rotten tree', Touchstone's metaphor of fruit ripening and rotting, or Jaques' suggestion that the duke should weed his 'better judgments of all opinion that grows rank in them'; and it would be hard to say how strongly and yet how subtly our feeling of being out of doors, of wind and weather, is increased or reinforced by such remarks as Adam's comparison of his age to

> a lusty winter,
> Frosty, but kindly;

Jaques' demand for

> as large a charter as the wind,
> To blow on whom I please;

Hymen's doggerel chant,

> You and you are sure together,
> As the winter to foul weather;

Rosalind's taunt to Silvius foolishly following Phoebe,

> Like foggy south, puffing with wind and rain,

or her gay defiance to Orlando, 'men are April when they woo, December when they wed: maids are May when they are maids, but the sky changes when they are wives'. . . .

THE TAMING OF THE SHREW

The Taming of the Shrew has comparatively few images, but, rather contrary to what we should expect, a high proportion—nearly one half—of poetical ones, counterbalancing the farce and roughness of the play, with touches of beauty. These are largely due to Petruchio, who uses close on one half of all the images in the play (40 out of 92), for he is a young man of keen perceptions, and observation of nature, and, when he chooses, he speaks with a poet's tongue.

Some of them he uses of Kate in irony:

> Say that she frown; I'll say she looks as clear
> As morning roses newly wash'd with dew.

> Kate like the hazel-twig
> Is straight and slender, and as brown in hue
> As hazel-nuts and sweeter than the kernels.

Some are frankly farcical, as when he rhapsodises over Vincentio's 'heavenly face'; or braggadocio, as when he swears that so long as he can find a rich wife, he cares not

> were she as rough
> As are the swelling Adriatic seas:
> ... though she chide as loud
> As thunder when the clouds in autumn crack.

Some are more formal and used of set purpose, throwing light on his attitude towards Kate, and the principle of his conduct, as when he speaks of her as a falcon which has to be starved before she can be tamed and trained, and who needs watching,

> as we watch these kites[15]
> That bate and beat and will not be obedient.

Some are little country pictures, brought in on occasion with tremendous effect of contrast, as when he turns on Gremio, describing all the terrifying noises he has heard, lions roaring, the sea raging, cannon booming in the field, thunder in the skies,

> And do you tell me of a woman's tongue,
> That gives not half so great a blow to hear
> As will a chestnut in a farmer's fire?

Another gives a glimpse of what doubtless was a common sight in country towns, or in the London of the day, in his bland query, when he arrives for his wedding, arrayed like a broken-down tinker,

> And wherefore gaze this goodly company,
> As if they saw some wondrous monument,
> Some comet or unusual prodigy?

and some seem to be just his natural, gay, imaginative speech, as when he answers Hortensio's query as to 'what happy gale' blows him to Padua, with

> Such wind as scatters young men through the world,
> To seek their fortunes farther than at home.

... Thoughtful poetry and strange brilliance, with a touch of the bizarre, are curiously expressive of the peculiar character and mental atmosphere of the play[s], and help towards the impression left on us of majesty and squalor, of thoughtful gravity and jeering cynicism, of the strange contradictions in life and still stranger contradictions in human nature, with its unexpected flaws and weaknesses and strengths and heroisms.

15. inferior hawks

CHAPTER 2

Shakespeare's Early Comedies

READINGS ON
THE COMEDIES

The Comedy of Errors Is a Farce

Francis Fergusson

Francis Fergusson discusses *The Comedy of Errors* as a farce based on a Roman comedy Shakespeare may have studied in his youth. According to Fergusson, Shakespeare modified the old form: Instead of a single set of identical twins, Shakespeare added another set to serve as servants to the lost twins, thus complicating the plot with more mistaken identities. Fergusson stresses the need to play this comedy straight; when all of the characters are deadly serious about their confusion, the audience, which knows the true situation, laughs harder. Fergusson also notes Shakespeare's use of a long-lost family to play on the sentimental hope for reunification. Fergusson concludes that Shakespeare reused the form of mistaken identity he established in *The Comedy of Errors* when he wrote his later comedies. Francis Fergusson was a theater director, educator, editor, and author of poetry, plays, and criticism. He taught literature and drama at Bennington College, Princeton University, Rutgers University, and Indiana University. He is the author of *Trope and Allegory: Themes Common to Dante and Shakespeare* and *The Idea of a Theatre: A Study of Ten Plays.*

The Comedy of Errors may have been written as early as 1589, but there is nothing about it to suggest the clumsiness of youth. It is an almost perfect farce of a Latin type, and (granted a reasonably good performance) it will produce laughter with the infallibility of a machine. This may not be so evident as one reads it for the first time. Like all comedy in this tradition, *The Comedy of Errors* reveals its true quality only in the theater.

From Francis Fergusson, *Shakespeare: The Pattern in His Carpet* (New York: Delacorte Press, 1970). Copyright 1970 by Francis Fergusson.

The play is based upon a Roman comedy, Plautus' *Menaechmi*, which in turn was derived from a still older Greek play. Shakespeare must have become familiar with Plautus when he was a boy in Stratford, for that author was read in Latin, and sometimes staged, in the Elizabethan schools. The young Shakespeare was, I suppose, looking for a reliable plot for his maiden effort in comedy, and the *Menaechmi*, whose comic situations were at least two thousand years old, had stood the test of time: Plautus was much relished in Shakespeare's England. In adapting the *Menaechmi*, he may have taken a few ideas from another play of Plautus', the *Amphitruo*; and for the prologue and the dénouement he used the romantic story of old Egeon and his long-lost family, which he had probably read in Gower's *Confessio Amantis*.

The situation on which the farce is based is improbable, simple, and absurd. Identical twins, both named Antipholus, were separated in their infancy when their family was shipwrecked. One was brought up in Ephesus,[1] the other in Syracuse,[2] and when the play opens Antipholus of Syracuse is in Ephesus searching for his long-lost brother. The errors of the title arise when the wife and friends of Antipholus of Ephesus confuse him with his Syracusan brother, of whom they have never heard. All of this is straight from the *Menaechmi*; but Shakespeare outdoes his Latin master by providing the identical Antipholuses with identical twins for servants, the two Dromios. The indistinguishable Dromios multiply the possibilities of error, and of course they make the situation still more wildly improbable. Plautus, with his single set of interchangeable twins, tries to make the coincidences credible, while his two young men keep crossing each other's paths without ever meeting. But Shakespeare has a different attitude. By exaggerating and overdoing coincidence he seems to be inviting us to laugh at the whole silly plot; yet at the same time he exploits each situation as though it were real: makes-believe it with a perfectly straight face. Thereby he makes his play both more elaborate and more lightly agile than Plautus'.

A PLOT BASED ON MISTAKEN IDENTITIES

The structure of the plot is much admired by critics, and rightly so. Shakespeare must be given full credit for it, be-

1. an ancient city of Greek Asia Minor, now Turkey   2. a city in southeast Sicily, Italy

cause, though the basic situation and some of the incidents are in Plautus, Shakespeare had to rearrange everything when he added the identical Dromios; and the sequence of incidents that gives the play its form and its ceaseless comic movement is his. He involves the two Antipholuses and the two Dromios as closely as possible in each other's affairs, yet he is obliged to keep the twins from actually meeting, for that would clear up all the errors instantly, and so end the play. The characters in the play must never know, until the end, why they are so frustrated, but the audience must be clear all along which Antipholus and which Dromio they are seeing, if they are to enjoy the mounting bewilderment of the Ephesians.

WIT IN *THE COMEDY OF ERRORS*

Farce in part derives its humor from puns and other kinds of wordplay. A brief example of the cross talk between Dromio of Syracuse and his master illustrates the play's elaborate wit.

ANT. S. If you will jest with me, know my aspéct,[1]
And fashion your demeanor to my looks,
Or I will beat this method in your sconce.[2]   34

DRO.S. Sconce call you it? So[3] you would leave battering, I had rather have it a head. An[4] you use these blows long, I must get a sconce for my head, and insconce[5] it too, or else I shall seek my wit in my shoulders. But, I pray, sir, why am I beaten?   40

ANT. S. Dost thou not know?

DRO. S. Nothing, sir, but that I am beaten.

ANT. S. Shall I tell you why?

DRO. S. Aye, sir, and wherefore; for they say every why hath a wherefore.   45

ANT. S. Why, first—for flouting me; and then, wherefore—For urging it the second time to me.

DRO. S. Was there ever any man thus beaten out of season,[6]
When in the why and the wherefore is neither rhyme nor reason?
Well, sir, I thank you.   50

ANT. S. Thank me, sir! For what?

DRO. S. Marry, sir, for this something that you gave me for nothing.

ANT. S. I'll make you amends next, to give you nothing for something.

1. look   2. (a) a head (b) a small military strongpoint   3. if only   4. if
5. seek protection within   6. at the wrong time

Every scene in the play (except for the first, a prologue devoted to old father Egeon's misfortunes) is based on a mistake in identity. And yet, on this extremely simple situation, Shakespeare builds mounting excitement, and the appearance of variety, as more and more characters are added to the confusion without ever quite clearing up the error. We watch the fun as we might a juggling act, in which more and more balls are tossed into the air: we know that a single slip will bring the whole effect down with a crash. Or one might compare the structure of the play to a "round," or "catch," which was very popular in Shakespeare's time: the simple device of bringing more and more singers in with the same tune can produce an effect of variety and excitement like that of the play. In the play this comical fugue reaches a climax in act 3, scene 1, when Antipholus of Ephesus and his Dromio are refused admission to their own house, while his brother from Syracuse and his Dromio are feasting within. It reaches a second climax in act 4, when all the characters have been drawn into a madly deluded chase through the streets of Ephesus; and this chase continues until the dénouement in act 5, when the twins finally meet.

CHARACTERS AS TYPES

In this play Shakespeare followed Plautus' light, amusing, and superficial style of character-drawing. In classical comedy it is assumed that human nature is incorrigible in its greeds, vices, and follies; that there are only a few human types; and that everyone can recognize them at once. Plautus' Menaechmus (Shakespeare's Antipholus) is simply the standard young citizen with the standard set of associates: scolding wife, grasping courtesan, shameless parasite, impudent servingman, and a few friends, other merchants with whom he has business.

Shakespeare slightly changed Plautus' cast for his London audience. He omitted the parasite, presumably because that ubiquitous figure of classical comedy was not labeled as such in London. He added the wife's sister (Luciana) and expanded the part of the wife herself (Adriana). In Plautus the wife is only a tough scold, and the husband treats her and his courtesan with the same frank cynicism. Shakespeare's Antipholus and Adriana are less hard and cold than their Roman forebears; but they too are presented as familiar types, not as individuals whose sufferings we are supposed to understand and share. The fact that Adriana weeps copiously when she is not scolding has led some critics to think Shakespeare meant us to take her seriously. But Luciana is on hand at once (act 2, scene 1) to make us see her as laughably childish: "Fie how impatience lowereth in your face," she says; and at the end (act 5) the Abbess sums her up: "Thy jealous fits/ Hath scared thy husband from the use of wits." In farce of this kind it ruins everything to sympathize with the characters. Adriana is presented as the eternal, incurably discontented wife; we are expected to laugh at her tantrums just as we do at the beatings the Antipholuses administer to their yelling Dromios.

Every situation, ridiculous though it appears to the audience, must be played straight, for if it is not, the whole structure of make-believe collapses: the Ephesians do not know why they are continually frustrated, and do not find their frustrations a bit amusing. The motivation of this play is like that of all classical comedy: everyone is pursuing pleasure and/or money. We must see the Ephesians busy with these serious pursuits when "the boys from Syracuse" come to town, and they must try their best to continue them even when they are involved in the mistakes which the Syracusans so unintentionally produce. Actors who try to be amusing, instead of relying on the situations, make the play intolerably slow, heavy, and "cute."

FARCE SOFTENED WITH ROMANCE

The Comedy of Errors is the purest—the most consistent—of Shakespeare's farces; and yet he frames it, between the prologue and the dénouement, in the story of old Egeon and his long-lost family, a romantic narrative filled with nostalgia and "sweet sadness." Perhaps he felt the need to soften the impact of the hard old Latin piece, in order to fit the taste of his English popular audience. The formula for our own popular entertainment includes a dose of sentimentality at the end, to top off an evening of broad and bawdy humor. Classical taste prefers the single tone, and from this point of view the framework that Shakespeare added to Plautus' comedy might seem a blemish. But we can see, in the light of Shakespeare's later work, that he was feeling his way toward the more many-sided vision and the subtler art of his maturity, when he learned how to harmonize the laughable and the lyric.

In later years Shakespeare used some of the plot-devices of

The Comedy of Errors for different and much more "Shake-spearean" purposes. In the great comedies of romance, *A Midsummer Night's Dream, As You Like It, Much Ado,* and *Twelfth Night,* he depends on mistaken identity almost as much as he does in this play; but the young lovers in the later plays fall into absurd errors not only because they don't know the facts, but because their visions are distorted by their own green terrors and longings, and must be matured and en-lightened before they can see clearly. At the beginning of his final phase Shakespeare returned to the story of Egeon and his lost family, and made out of it that strange play, *Pericles, Prince of Tyre,* which is, among other things, a parable of in-nocence and experience in the course of a whole generation.

If one remembers these later works one can see more clearly just what Shakespeare's intention was in *The Comedy of Errors.* He sets it all in the streets of Ephesus, a place as public and objective as a baseball diamond or a chess board. There is no need there for psychology or individual portraiture to understand what happens; and because we never share the feelings or emotionally colored perceptions of any of the characters, there is no room for lyric poetry. The characters never learn anything but the facts, never come to understand themselves or each other any better than they did at first; and the audience is not offered any new insights either, but is simply invited to laugh once more at incurable, familiar human folly. Shakespeare accepted the strict limitations of style and of medium that define the con-vention of classical comedy. And he made not only an inde-structible entertainment but (what is less evident at first) an elegant theatrical form.

Serious Themes in *The Comedy of Errors*

R.A. Foakes

R.A. Foakes argues that serious themes lie beneath the farcical actions of *The Comedy of Errors*. He says that the suffering caused by characters' confusion and dislocation evokes sympathy, especially for Egeon and the servants, who are helpless and abused. In addition, Foakes shows how disorder suggests the presence of witchcraft, a thread carried through the play as characters search for a power responsible for their bizarre experiences. Finally, the disruption of both family and community leads to a sense of evil at work, suggested by such words as *fiend* and *Satan*. Foakes concludes that the fun in the play cannot be missed, but sympathy for the dislocated and the urgent need for order might be. R.A. Foakes has taught English at University College, Toronto, and the University of Kent, England. He has edited numerous volumes of Shakespeare's plays and published *Shakespeare: The Dark Comedies to the Last Plays: From Satire to Celebration.*

In introducing Luciana, Egeon, and Emilia, Shakespeare, it is argued, brought in a 'range of sentiment utterly incompatible with the atmosphere of *The Comedy of Errors*', a play in which the general temper of life is 'crude, coarse and brutal'. A different view has been taken of the play, more especially in recent years. Perhaps Dowden was the first to be so moved by the plight of Egeon. . . . What he recognized is that in spite of the implausibility and fantastic coincidences of Egeon's tale of the shipwreck, we are directly affected by his wretchedness, his dramatic presence on stage as a lonely, pathetic figure, lacking money and friends, and sentenced to die at the day's end. . . .

From R.A. Foakes, ed., *The Comedy of Errors*, Arden Edition of the Works of William Shakespeare (London: Methuen, 1962). Reprinted by permission of Routledge, UK.

The note of weirdness and bewitchment that runs through the comic action is one of the features of the play that has received serious attention.... Another feature that has been well brought out is the interplay between personal and commercial relationships, in which 'giving' ultimately triumphs over 'taking and keeping'—and, one might add, over paying.... The discords and final harmony in human relationships are reflected in images of disorder and order, and the sense of witchcraft in Ephesus has a bearing here as related to disorder. The recognition of these aspects of the play has led to the just claim that 'it is a play of greater promise than the mere dexterity of its plotting suggests'....

THE INITIAL CONFUSION

So Antipholus of Syracuse arrives in Ephesus[1] with a feeling that in searching for his mother and brother he has lost his identity, as if he will only find himself when he finds them:

> I to the world am like a drop of water
> That in the ocean seeks another drop,
> Who, falling there to find his fellow forth,
> (Unseen, inquisitive) confounds himself.
> So I, to find a mother and a brother,
> In quest of them, unhappy, lose myself.   (act 1, scene 2)

Ephesus holds a shock for him, mistaking him for his twin, and fastens an identity on him, so that he is invited to dine with Adriana as her husband, and feels that he is

> Known unto these, and to myself disguis'd.   (act 2, scene 2)

Here he seizes on the status of intimacy given to him in the household to make love to Luciana, and in her finds a new self, as he discovers a true passion for her. When he says,

> would you create me new?
> Transform me then, and to your power I'll yield,
> (act 3, scene 2)

he is already transformed through love, in the recognition that she is

> mine own self's better part,
> Mine eye's clear eye, my dear heart's dearer heart.
> (act 3, scene 2)

Luciana thinks he is her brother-in-law gone mad, and, in the face of her inability to recognize him for what he is, he finally claims, 'I am thee'.

---

1. an ancient city in Greek Asia Minor, today Turkey

Even as Antipholus of Syracuse[2] discovers a new self, he is also bewildered by the assumptions of the people he meets, including Luciana, that they know him, that he is another person. Meanwhile, his brother, Antipholus of Ephesus, a more strongly determined character, more certain of himself, is angered when his wife refuses to acknowledge his identity; and Adriana, by nature jealous of him, and misled by his twin's attempt to woo Luciana, comes to think the worst of her husband, until she is ready to transform him in her mind:

> He is deformed, crooked, old and sere,
> Ill-fac'd, worse bodied, shapeless everywhere;
> Vicious, ungentle, foolish, blunt, unkind,
> Stigmatical in making, worse in mind.   (act 4, scene 2)

It is but a step from this for her to treat him as if he were mad or possessed, make him endure the ministrations of Doctor Pinch, and have him locked away in a dark cellar.

THE ABUSE OF THE SERVANTS

The serious force of the presentation of the Antipholus twins is paralleled by a more comic treatment of their servants. Each is puzzled at being mistaken for the other, and each comes to feel that he is being transformed—but into an ass, rather than another person. So Dromio of Ephesus suffers like an ass from the blows of his master, and, finding that another has assumed his office and identity as servant in Adriana's household, and that for his service he is rewarded with still more blows as his master grows angrier, he resigns himself to his topsy-turvy world with a humorous acceptance of it:

> EPH. ANT. Thou art sensible in nothing but blows, and so is an ass.
>
> EPH. DRO. I am an ass indeed; you may prove it by my long ears. I have served him from the hour of my nativity to this instant, and have nothing at his hands for my service but blows . . .   (act 4, scene 4)

At the same time, Dromio of Syracuse shares something of his master's sense of being subjected to witchcraft, and when Luciana, whom he has never seen before, addresses him by name, he speaks as if he has been 'transformed':

> SYR. DRO. I am transformed, master, am I not?

2. an ancient city in southeast Sicily, Italy

SYR. ANT. I think thou art in mind, and so am I.

SYR. DRO. Nay, master, both in mind and in my shape.

SYR. ANT. Thou hast thine own form.

SYR. DRO.   No, I am an ape.

LUC. If thou art chang'd to aught, 'tis to an ass.

SYR. DRO. 'Tis true, she rides me, and I long for grass;
'Tis so, I am an ass. . . .   (act 2, scene 2)

His sense of change or loss of identity is confirmed when the
kitchen-maid Nell treats him as her man, and he bursts out,
'I am an ass, I am a woman's man, and besides myself'. Each
Dromio applies the term 'ass' in relation to the beatings he
is made to suffer, and to the way he is made to seem a fool;
but the idea of being made a beast operates more generally
in the play, reflecting the process of passion overcoming reason, as an animal rage, fear, or spite seizes on each of the
main characters.

THE DISRUPTION OF FAMILY AND COMMUNITY

For the sense of loss or change of identity in these figures
goes together with a disruption of family, personal, and social relationships. Antipholus of Syracuse loses himself in
the search for his mother and brother, but is hailed by all in
Ephesus as if they knew him well; even as he thinks he is
subject to 'imaginary wiles', he is, unwittingly, causing a rift
in the marriage of Adriana and his brother, and stirring discord between Antipholus of Ephesus and, on the one hand
Angelo the goldsmith, on the other hand the Courtesan, over
the matter of the chain. In the confusion which follows upon
his dining with Adriana, the new self he had found in his
passion for Luciana is frustrated; confirmed in his belief that
he wanders in 'illusions', he comes on at the end of act 4,
sword in hand, to drive her and Adriana off as 'witches'. At
the same time, Antipholus of Ephesus, denied entry to his
own house, comes to believe that he is the victim of a plot,
and that his wife is a 'strumpet'. In addition, the normal relationship of master and servant is broken as each Antipholus meets the other's Dromio, and then beats his own servant for failing to carry out orders given to someone else.
The normal intercourse of the city in its friendly, commercial relationships is also disturbed, to the extent that the Second Merchant, believing himself wronged, puts both Angelo

and Antipholus under arrest, and the long-standing trust between these two is destroyed. The confusions of identity, involving for Antipholus of Syracuse and the two Dromios a sense especially of loss or transformation, and for Antipholus of Ephesus a need defiantly to assert his identity in a world that seems to go mad, thus lead to a breakdown of the social order through the frustration of normal relationships. Quarrels and arrests follow; Antipholus of Ephesus is bound and locked up; Doctor Pinch is harshly treated, and suffers the painful loss of a beard; the Dromios are mercilessly beaten; and Antipholus of Syracuse and his Dromio usurp the office of the law when they rush in with 'naked swords'.

THE ASSOCIATION OF WITCHCRAFT

The growth of this disorder is reflected in two other strands in language and action which reinforce the serious undertones of the comedy. One is the establishment of Ephesus as a place associated with witchcraft. Antipholus of Syracuse arrives there with a prejudice about the city:[3]

> They say this town is full of cozenage,
> As nimble jugglers that deceive the eye,
> Dark-working sorcerers that change the mind,
> Soul-killing witches that deform the body,
> Disguised cheaters, prating mountebanks,
> And many such-like liberties of sin.   (act 1, scene 2)

As he becomes involved with the Merchant, Adriana, Luciana, and the Courtesan, so his belief that the city is a nest of sorcerers grows stronger. He wonders if his love for Luciana results from bewitchment, and calls her 'mermaid' and 'siren'; soon he is ready to think 'There's none but witches do inhabit here', or 'Lapland sorcerers'; he comes to regard the Courtesan as a 'fiend' and a 'sorceress', and finally achieves a state of mind so distraught that he feels safe only with a sword in his hand, and, pursued by Adriana's men, takes refuge in the priory. The prejudice which he has on reaching Ephesus provides a ready explanation for all the strange things that happen to him, and becomes a settled conviction; he is more and more disabled from distinguishing between what is real and what is not, until the whole city seems to him to be in the grip of an evil power:

> This fellow is distract, and so am I,

---

3. Shakespeare deliberately set the scene of his play in Ephesus because of the city's biblical associations with sorcery.

And here we wander in illusions—
Some blessed power deliver us from hence!   (act 4, scene 3)

Antipholus of Ephesus, by contrast, regards himself as alone sane in a world gone mad. He is given some force of character, and a tendency to violence, so that when he is shut out of his own house, he is driven to bewilderment and to passionate exclamation; though calmed for a moment by Balthasar, he thinks of punishing his wife by going at once to the Courtesan's, and by bestowing a 'rope's end', i.e. a whipping, upon Adriana and her 'confederates'. He invents an explanation of her treatment of him with this word; he decides he is the victim of a conspiracy. This private interpretation of his experience is confirmed for him when he is arrested in error, meets Dromio of Syracuse at cross-purposes, in his anger is himself regarded as mad, bewitched, or possessed, and is at last imprisoned in a 'dark and dankish vault'.

THE ASSOCIATION OF EVIL

The confusions of identity and consequent disruptions of normal relationships force the characters to judge events according to their own private ordering of experience, as Adriana, too, is ready, at the suggestion of the Courtesan, to think her husband mad, and treat him as a dangerous lunatic. Out of the clashes of these private worlds of experience emerges another strand in language and action which is of some importance, a sense of evil at work in Ephesus. Dromio of Syracuse jests about the Officer who arrests Antipholus of Ephesus, calling him a devil,

One that, before the judgment, carries poor souls to hell;
(act 4, scene 2)

he is quibbling on the last judgment, and on a common term for prison, but his jest, as is characteristic of the word-play of the Dromios, quickly becomes earnest when he meets his own master in the next scene. For Antipholus of Syracuse really thinks of the Courtesan as a 'fiend', and uses to her Christ's words, 'Satan, avoid', spoken in rejection of the devil's temptations in the wilderness;[4] and if the Officer was a 'devil in an everlasting garment' to Dromio, the Courtesan now becomes 'the devil's dam'. A little later, Adriana puts her husband, as a man possessed by the 'fiend', into the

---

4. *Matthew*, iv. 10 (Geneva version)

hands of an exorcist, who chants,

> I charge thee, Satan, hous'd within this man,
> To yield possession to my holy prayers.   (act 4, scene 4)

These hints of the devil at work mark a stage in the play when the appearance of normal order breaks down, and the action erupts into violence, as one Antipholus is bound, and the other rushes in to attack a group he believes are 'witches'—a group that includes the Officer of the law.

CHAOS BEFORE ORDER IS RESTORED

In act 5 the scene transfers to the Priory, which is the setting for the resolution of all difficulties, and which lends a faintly holy and redeeming colour to the end of the play. Here the enveloping action concerning Egeon is resumed. His hopeless condition, stranded friendless in a hostile city where the law condemned him to death, had been presented in a simple and dignified way in the opening scene. The Duke, representative of justice, had listened to the tale of his long search for his family, and had given him a day in which to seek, vainly as we see, for money to pay a ransom that would save him from execution. The end of the day comes just when one Antipholus lies bound as a madman, and the other has taken refuge in the Priory. At this point, a solemn procession enters, headed by the Duke, and bringing on Egeon, bound, guarded, and accompanied by the executioner. Adriana, who is anxiously trying to persuade the Abbess to release the man she thinks to be her husband, stops the Duke to beg for 'Justice, most sacred Duke, against the Abbess', and, shortly afterwards, Antipholus of Ephesus arrives to cry, 'Justice, most gracious Duke, O, grant me justice', this time against Adriana. Each clamours for an idea of justice based on a private ordering of experience, and the conflicting evidence of witnesses and supporters sets a problem too difficult for the law to solve; the Duke cries,

> Why, what an intricate impeach is this?
> I think you all have drunk of Circe's cup.[5]   (act 5, scene 1)

His words nicely suggest the kind and degree of transformation that has taken place in the citizens of Ephesus; they are behaving madly, and there is no order or coherence in what they allege against one another.

---

5. in Greek mythology, a witch who turned Odysseus's men into swine, who inwardly remained men

To make matters worse, Egeon seizes the opportunity to appeal for help to the son he sees before him, but Antipholus of Ephesus does not know him. The law cannot deal with this situation, and it is time for the Abbess to reappear, with the second Antipholus; the twins are brought face to face for the first time, Adriana's mistake is revealed, and Egeon is saved as the Abbess turns out to be his long-lost wife Emilia. It is as if, through her intervention, the harsh justice embodied in the Duke is tempered by a Christian grace and mercy. Bitterness gives way to harmony, a harmony celebrated in a feast that marks a new beginning, a new life, a baptismal feast, from which Antipholus of Ephesus will not be excluded. Here the characters recover or discover their real identity, order is restored, and the two pairs of twins follow the others off stage, the masters embracing, the servants hand in hand. Violence is replaced by mildness and love, and the sense of witchcraft, evil, and Circean transformation is dispelled.

In this account of the play, I have laid stress on its serious elements, but not out of any desire to minimize its comic appeal, its clever exploitation of mistakes, of repartee, and talk at cross-purposes. The fact is that the serious elements are in some danger of going unobserved, while no one is likely to miss the fun. . . .

The play has farcical comedy, and it has fantasy, but it does more than merely provoke laughter, or release us temporarily from inhibitions and custom into a world free as a child's, affording delight and freshening us up. It also invites compassion, a measure of sympathy, and a deeper response to the disruption of social and family relationships which the action brings about. Our concern for the Antipholus twins, for Adriana and Luciana, and our sense of disorder are deepened in the context of suffering provided by the enveloping action.

The Taming of the Shrew Is a Farce

Mark Van Doren

Mark Van Doren declares Shakespeare's *The Taming of the Shrew* is a farce, not a romance. Van Doren acknowledges that Petruchio's treatment of Katharina is brutal, behavior that decent and sensitive people would find offensive. Van Doren also acknowledges that audiences have been laughing through this play for four centuries. According to Van Doren, the play's structure as a farce saves it from cruelty. A farce insulates the audience from concern about people and redirects their attention to exaggerated and unexpected devices. Moreover, Shakespeare's lusty, vigorous language also draws the attention of the audience away from the feelings of the characters. Since Katharina and Petruchio are equally matched and gradually develop affection for each other as they battle, the audience feels absolved of concern about mistreatment. Mark Van Doren taught English at Columbia University in New York for many years. He published poems, short stories, and critical works on English poet John Dryden and on American writers E.A. Robinson, Henry David Thoreau, and Nathaniel Hawthorne.

When Petruchio the woman-hater is asked what gale blows him from Verona to Padua he answers airily, being a free and happy fellow with no other care than the need to find himself a wealthy wife:

> Such wind as scatters young men through the world
> To seek their fortunes farther than at home
> Where small experience grows.   (act 1, scene 2)

The hilarious piece of which he is hero might so far, then, be such an excursion into the romantic universe of young Italian adventure as "The Two Gentlemen of Verona" is; for that experiment, of about the same age as "The Shrew," starts also with youthful blades whetting their edges on the wheel of travel.

THE TAMING OF THE SHREW IS A FARCE

But Petruchio is hero of a farce, not of a romance. Comedy is made once more from situation: a shrew is to be tamed, a man is found to tame her, and he proceeds to do so by as many devices as can be developed in the time available. The interest of the audience will be in the devices, not in the persons who work them or upon whom they are worked. A certain callousness will be induced to form in the sensibilities of the beholder, so that whereas in another case he would be outraged he will now laugh freely and steadily for two hours. The practitioner in farce, no less than the practitioner in melodrama, must possess the art of insulating his audience's heart so that it cannot be shocked while the machinery hums.

"The Taming of the Shrew," however, has a deep and curious interest such as "The Comedy of Errors" nowhere has. Formally it is as much a farce, and leans as frankly on a doctrine which Shakespeare must have adopted in cold blood, for on the evidence of the other plays it was not his own. This is the doctrine of male superiority, which Luciana had expressed in "The Comedy of Errors" when she reminded Adriana that men "are masters to their females," (II, i, 24), and which Petruchio expresses here not only when he declares of Katherine that

> She is my goods, my chattels; she is my house,
> My household stuff, my field, my barn,
> My horse, my ox, my ass, my any thing.   (act 3, scene 2)

but indeed at all times and by all his actions; nor does Katherine fail at the end to agree. Yet the resulting play, as its popularity attests, is strangely and permanently interesting.

This is because it has hit the relation of the sexes at its livest point. Shakespeare hit the point again, and classically for him, in the story of Beatrice and Benedick; but even now he is master of the theme that lies in the war between love and pride, in the perhaps perversely fascinating spectacle of intellect and will being brought into line with instinct. Love stories are never so engaging as when their principals do not wish to love, and particularly when it is their power that prevents them. For one thing, we are never so sure as then that love is genuine; and for another, there is a peculiar delight in discovering that two persons have mistaken attraction for repulsion, and in listening to the reverse language of raillery which they employ in place of lisps and sighs. The best lovers are witty lovers who bury their perturbation under abuse; at least this is true for comedy, and by all means it is the case where situation is the thing.

COMEDY MELDS WITH FARCE

Definitions of various kinds of comedy tend to overlap. Farce, not an exclusive form, has elements of low comedy, such as quarreling, fighting, noisy singing, boisterous conduct, and boasting, as well as elements of serious comedy. In A Handbook to Literature, *William Flint Thrall, Addison Hibbard, and C. Hugh Holman explain.*

Farce: . . . In France, *farce* meant any sort of extemporaneous addition in a play, especially comic jokes or "gags," the clownish actors speaking "more than was set down" for them. In the late seventeenth century *farce* was used in England to mean any short humorous play, as distinguished from regular five-act COMEDY. The development in these plays of certain elements of LOW COMEDY is responsible for the usual modern meaning of *farce:* a dramatic piece intended to excite laughter and depending less on PLOT and character than on exaggerated, improbable situations, the humor arising from gross incongruities, coarse wit, or horseplay. *Farce* merges into COMEDY, and the same play (e.g., Shakespeare's *The Taming of the Shrew*) may be called by some a *farce*, by others a COMEDY. . . .

Farce-Comedy: A term sometimes applied to comedies which rely for their interest chiefly on farcical devices, but which contain some truly comic elements which elevate them above most FARCE. Shakespeare's *The Taming of the Shrew* and *The Merry Wives of Windsor* are called *farce-comedies* by some authorities.

Our secret occupation as we watch "The Taming of the Shrew" consists of noting the stages by which both Petruchio and Katherine—both of them, for in spite of everything the business is mutual—surrender to the fact of their affection. Shakespeare has done this not by violating his form, not by forgetting at any point to write farce, and least of all by char-

acterizing his couple. He has left them man and woman, figures for whom we can substitute ourselves, and that is precisely what we do as we commence to understand why
Katherine wants so badly to hear Bianca talk of her suitors,
even beats her because she will not; as we read reservations
into her scorn of Petruchio; as we wait to see her give Petruchio (v, i) his first quiet kiss; and as we assume behind
Petruchio's roughness a growing attachment to this woman
he is so deliciously—we must confess it—torturing. Shakespeare has done what he has done somewhat as a general
takes a city: by sheer strength, in utter confidence, and with
the soundest knowledge of our outstanding weakness.

THE PLAY'S VIGOROUS LANGUAGE

Both the man and the woman are brilliant of tongue. She can
call him "a mad-cap ruffian and a swearing Jack," "a frantic
fool," "a mad-brain rudesby." But his high spirits carry him
as far as genius. His anger, real or pretended, leads him to
the limits of language:

> You peasant swain! You whoreson malt-horse drudge![1]
>
> . . . .
>
> A whoreson beetle-headed,[2] flap-ear'd knave!
>
> . . . .
>
> Why, this was moulded on a porringer.[3] . . .
> Why, 't is a cockle[4] or a walnut-shell,
> A knack, a toy, a trick, a baby's cap.
>
> . . . .
>
> Why, thou say'st true; it is a paltry cap,
> A custard-coffin,[5] a bauble, a silken pie.
>
> . . . .
>
> What's this? A sleeve?[6] 'T is like a demi-cannon.[7]
> What, up and down, carv'd like an apple-tart?
> Here's snip and nip and cut and slish and slash,
> Like to a censer[8] in a barber's shop.

The language of the play, or at any rate of the play as it concerns Katherine and Petruchio, is everywhere vigorous and
vernacular, and healthily grown over with tough local
terms. We hear of a chestnut in a farmer's fire, of boys with

---

1. horse which trudges round and round turning a grain mill   2. with a head like a
wooden pile-driving hammer   3. basin   4. cockle shell   5. a custard pie   6. sleeves
were separate and attached with pins   7. large cannon   8. pot with a perforated lid
for burning perfume

bugs, of hazel-twigs and hazel nuts, of kersey boot-hose, of horses shoulder-shotten[9] and begnawn with the bots,[10] of sops[11] thrown in the sexton's face, of apples and oysters, of a bottom of brown thread, of rush-candles, and of parsley in the garden to stuff a rabbit. Petruchio's crowning harangue against the tailor is stuck as full of such terms as a ham with cloves:

> Thou liest, thou thread, thou thimble,
> Thou yard, three-quarters, half-yard, quarter, nail![12]
> Thou flea, thou nit, thou winter-cricket[13] thou! . . .
> Away, thou rag, thou quantity,[14] thou remnant.
>
> (act 4, scene 3)

But the servants also are accomplished in the speech of their region, which it goes without saying is not Italy. . . .

But the comedy has never strayed from its path, unless the insipid second story of Bianca and her suitors is to be considered an attempt, by Shakespeare or by someone else, to save the whole for romance. It is not saved. A play in which the heroine can be called a devil, a wench, a fiend of hell, a rotten apple, a thing to be boarded, an irksome brawling scold, a wildcat, and in which we nevertheless take the purest pleasure, has in fact been saved, but saved as farce. How otherwise could we behold so callously the wringing of ears and the knocking of heads which appear to be Petruchio's natural habits—and his servants', and Katherine's, for she ties her sister's hands and strikes at least three persons before she settles down? As for the settling down, there is that last long speech of hers in which she declares the humble duty of a wife in terms which would be painful to us were she a person as Portia[15] and Imogen[16] are persons. Katherine is a shrew. She has been tamed. And the logic of farce is that she should say so.

---

9. dislocated in the shoulders   10. worms in the stomach   11. wine   12. creature as small and thin as a nail   13. starved and shriveled   14. piece of material   15. in *The Merchant of Venice*   16. in *Cymbeline*

An Understanding of Elizabethan Medicine Enlightens *The Taming of the Shrew*

John W. Draper

John W. Draper interprets the plot of *The Taming of the Shrew* in light of Renaissance medical history. Draper documents the traditional beliefs concerning the humors, the four body fluids thought to affect both a person's physical and psychological natures. He then relates them to Katharina's condition and Petruchio's cure. Katharina has too much bile, or choler, the cause of her shrewish behavior. According to Draper, Petruchio takes Katharina on a cold, wet journey, starves her, keeps her awake on her wedding night, and threatens to curtail her travel to her father's house—each action specifically designed to treat her choleric condition. Draper concludes that his medical interpretation explains difficulties critics have previously been unable to resolve about the play and allows audiences justification and even sympathy for the cruel scenes in the play. John W. Draper was professor of English at New York University, Bryn Mawr College in Pennsylvania, and Harvard University. He published *The Hamlet of Shakespeare's Audience*, *The Humors and Shakespeare's Characters*, and more than a hundred journal articles.

Katherina Minola should have been a charming and courtly young lady: she is depicted as the product of a culture—the culture of Renaissance Italy—that gave high praise and high reward to courtliness. Moreover, she is "fair"; she is "young and beauteous"; and, as her future husband somewhat plainly puts it, she is "a lusty wench." Her father's wealth and position, furthermore, have assured her of some cultural opportunities, at least in music; and, indeed, she has been "Brought up as best becomes a gentlewoman." She should be capable also in domestic matters; for her father as a widower would presumably depend on her to superintend his household: at least, she certainly knows enough to object to her husband's ill-treatment of his servants. All these accomplishments, Shakespeare develops far beyond his source, which merely groups her with her sisters as "fair dames"; but they are all to no purpose, for Katherine is a confirmed and violent shrew. She is "Renoun'd in Padua for her scolding tongue", and "Kate the curst"; even her father calls her a "shrew" and a "hilding of a devilish spirit." Her actions bear out this description: she drives her music-teacher from her with "vile terms"; and she ties her sister's hands and strikes her. In short, Kate's temper ruins all her good qualities.

In Shakespeare's source, Kate seems clearly to be acting a part: she intends either to "match" her future husband, or at least to test his "manhood" before she submits to his control. In Shakespeare's play, though Petruchio tries to excuse her as "curst" only "for policy," her violence is really part and parcel of her actual disposition; and indeed Shakespeare suggests the causes that produced it: the taunts of Hortensio, her natural jealousy of her sister who has suitors when she has none, and her father's peremptory manner of addressing her. She reproaches him with making her a "stale" or public laughingstock; and she bitterly resents the groom's late arrival at her wedding and his outrageous dress and ill-mannered speech and action even in the midst of the ceremony. Kate is proud and high-spirited; and, as she says, she has "never needed" that she "should entreat"; and apparently either by nature or through years of habit, she has come to get what she wants by making life miserable for those around her. Her violent humor is no mere pretense like that of Corporal Nym,[1] but an actual condition that is part of her very self.

PHYSICAL AND PSYCHOLOGICAL EFFECTS OF THE HUMORS

According to medical tradition, which came down to the Renaissance from Galen,[2] the body contained four "humors," or fluids: blood, a predominance of which made one sanguine;

1. a character in Shakespeare's *The Merry Wives of Windsor* and *Henry V*   2. a celebrated physician who lived in Asia Minor during the first century A.D. He wrote five hundred treatises on medicine. Other sources mentioned here are from Renaissance England.

phlegm, which made one slow or phlegmatic; bile (choler), which made one wrathful or choleric; and black bile (melancholy), which in extreme cases might produce a sort of manic-depressive psychosis. Bile, commonly called by its Greek name "choler," was supposed to be hot and dry. Elyot says that this heat is "kendlyd in the harte," and so courses throughout the body; and, according to Coeffeteau, it "enflames the blood and spirits, which are about the heart, by means of the gall, which in this heat exhales it selfe, and ascends vnto the braine, where it troubles our imagination." Walkington considers choler rather a disease of "the mouth of the stomach." A predominance of choler in the system, moreover, was supposed to produce a lean and muscular physique and numerous other bodily traits on which not all authorities agreed.

On its psychological effects, however, there was little disagreement. Choleric people were supposed to be "obstinate" and yet "inconsistent," "propt of wit," but given to "furie," and this last was their outstanding trait, and led to "chiding," or even to "murther, robbery, sedition." This humor, therefore, was appropriate to "All warriers, brawlers . . . theeues." Astrologers associated the type with the warlike planet Mars, which was considered an unlucky influence; and choleric people were generally feared and disliked. The Huguenot La Primaudaye, writing in a more moralistic vein, treats choler as a sin; and Coeffeteau considered it the most violent and dangerous of all the humors: the heat of choler is "full of bitterness," and "tends to the destruction of the object which it pursues" and those afflicted with the malady should be treated like "monsters and serpents" whom one should "strive to smother as soon as they are disclosed." Kate's violence of disposition clearly puts her in the choleric category; and Grumio, in trying to cure her, says that she must not have "choleric" food. Coeffeteau attributes to Aristotle a distinction between three types of choler: the first "sudden," a burst of anger such as anyone might have, rather than a bodily disease; the second, a smoldering hatred from a wrong; the third a protracted violence. Kate's symptoms point to the last of these three types; and, if this diagnosis be correct, truly her case was parlous.

Renaissance Women's Only Career Choice

In the Middle Ages, a young woman of position might select either of two careers: she might become the betrothed of

God by entering a convent, or she might take unto herself a human husband—or rather her father might select one for her. In the Renaissance, at least in England, but one career remained after the suppression of the monasteries, the career of marriage; and failure to get a husband brought on a girl the shame of spinsterhood. No wonder that "Katherine the curst" is mentioned in the play as the "worst" possible "title" for a maid; and that Kate bitterly resents Hortensio's fling, "No mates for you!" She may object to her father's choice of a husband for her, and, with a fine irony, call her future lord "a mad-brain rudesby full of spleen [violent anger]"; but, for all that, she knows that she is lucky to get any husband, and not "lead apes in hell." Grumio declares that she might best be mated to the devil, for her husband will "be married to hell"; but Petruchio more auspiciously compares his humor and hers to "two raging fires" that will the more quickly burn each other out. Indeed, marriage was considered the severest test for persons of the choleric type: Walkington thought that such were too "variable" to make a happy match; Coeffeteau warned them to avoid the company of other "quarrelsome persons"; and Ferrand considers the choleric the most unhappy in married life, especially if linked to another of its own complexion: "But if two Cholerick Persons meet together, this is rather a slavery then true Love, it is so subject to Outrages and Anger, notwithstanding the neerenesse of their coplexions." Indeed Katherine might deem herself lucky to get any husband at all; and Petruchio was taking a great chance.

In both Shakespeare and his source, Petruchio's violence is merely a role assumed for the occasion: his marrying of Kate in fact suggests that his actual temper must have been sanguine! He has a tough fibre; and, as Grumio predicts, "scolding" does "little good upon him." He seems to come from an impoverished country family; and having had his fling of travel and town life, he is ready to settle down and marry for money as a prudent gentleman should. He has decided that he will "tame" the girl and make her "Comformable to other household Kates."

PETRUCHIO'S CURE FOR KATHERINE'S CHOLER

His cure, while it lasts, is as violent as the disease, but he knows no "better" way; and, if anyone else does, let him tell it, for " 'Tis charity to show." As it is, however, he goes round

PETRUCHIO REVIEWS HIS TREATMENT PLAN

In his soliloquy in The Taming of the Shrew, *act 4, scene 1,
Petruchio describes how he plans to treat Katharina's "mad
and headstrong humor." The couple has married that morning and recently arrived at the country house.*

Thus have I politicly[1] begun my reign,
And 'tis my hope to end successfully.
My falcon[2] now is sharp and passing empty,
And till she stoop, she must not be full-gorged,
For then she never looks upon her lure.
Another way I have to man my haggard,
To make her come and know her keeper's call,
That is, to watch her, as we watch these kites
That bate, and beat, and will not be obedient.
She eat no meat today, nor none shall eat.
Last night she slept not, nor tonight she shall not.
As with the meat, some undeservèd fault
I'll find about the making of the bed,
And here I'll fling the pillow, there the bolster,
This way the coverlet, another way the sheets.
Aye, and amid this hurly[3] I intend[4]
That all is done in reverend care of her;
And in conclusion she shall watch all night.
And if she chance to nod, I'll rail and brawl
And with the clamor keep her still[5] awake.
This is a way to kill a wife with kindness,[6]
And thus I'll curb her mad and headstrong humor.
He that knows better how to tame a shrew
Now let him speak. 'Tis charity to show.

1. cunningly, shrewdly   2. Petruchio thus tries to train Katharina as if she
were a wild hawk   3. confusion   4. pretend   5. continuously   6. a proverb
meaning to spoil with overindulgence

to work; and, having wooed the lady with persistent good
humor, no matter what she said or did, he now weds her
with an equally persistent lunatic humor, and lets her do
and say what she will in the way of threat and entreaty. For
all its apparent lunacy, however, his treatment has basis in
medical and scientific theory. The disease had a "deepe
root," and so would require drastic treatment; and, to prepare himself for this most strenuous role, Petruchio might
well quaff off the customary sweet "muscadel" at his wedding, for sweet wines were especially supposed to augment
choler in the system, and he is planning to out-Herod Herod.

So Petruchio takes his wife in hand, determines to "curb her mad and headstrong humor"; he rails and rants at wedding-guests and servants; as Peter says, "He kills her in her own humor"; and, as if he were taming a hawk, he sees to it that she shall have little food or sleep: they leave the wedding before the banquet; she has no dinner, and no sleep that night. This is quite in the best tradition of Galen; for "much eating is also dangerful to this [choleric] humor." Choler, moreover, was very hot and dry; and, on the way home, Petruchio took care to expose his wife to mud and mire and cold, so that she arrived "almost frozen to death" at a cheerless house in which apparently the servants have not yet made the fire. Next day, she again complains of the "cold cheer." The weather suggests winter; and choler was supposed to have most of its power in the late spring and summer: just as Shakespeare changed the date of *Romeo and Juliet* to August so that "summer's ripening breath" might enhance the love of the two protagonists, so in *The Taming of the Shrew*, he adds to his source a description of the journey after the wedding with its detail of the cold, inclement season, for this was doubtless intended to play its part in the curing of Kate's choler.

In Shakespeare's source, Kate is denied mustard as "too choleric" a condiment: perhaps this passage gave Shakespeare his hint for the medical treatment of her case. At all events, he likewise has Grumio declare that mustard is "too hot" for her, and that she must avoid "choleric food." Shakespeare's Petruchio, furthermore, orders "burnt" meat off the table, and closely follows good medical tradition in declaring:

'Tis burnt; and so is all the meat.
What dogs are these! Where is the rascal cook?
How durst you, villains, bring it from the dresser . . .
I tell thee, Kate, 'twas burnt and dried away,
And I expressly am forbid to touch it,
For it engenders choler, planteth anger;
And better 'twere that *both of us did fast,*
Since, of ourselves, ourselves are choleric,[3]
Than feed it with such over-roasted flesh.

The ultimate insult is on the bridal night when she sits up while he improves the occasion by "making a sermon of continency to her." This is a wrong almost comparable to that of the forsaken Mariana in *Measure for Measure*; and yet

3. italics are Draper's

it also is a part of the therapeutic process; for choleric persons were supposed to be over-passionate. The last stage of the treatment was especially tantalizing: Walkington, following Galen, declares that much motion is bad for choleric people; and, when Petruchio and Katherine set out for her father's house, he threatens, at her every sign of choler or even at the slightest contradiction, to quit the journey and go back home; and the ability to stand rough travel without a return of her disorder was good proof of her cure. In short, Petruchio is not merely ill-treating his wife to break her spirit, but rather applying contemporary medical knowledge to combat her disease.

THE STEPS IN KATHERINE'S RECOVERY

The cure certainly justified this strenuous therapy, and Shakespeare traces the steps in her recovery by showing her change in psychological attitude. Kate's first reaction to her mad wooer is self-pity; and indeed even her father feels that Petruchio's treatment of her "would vex a saint." At the wedding, the bridegroom seems even "curster than she . . . a devil, a devil, a very fiend"; and she rebels when he hurries off before the nuptial feast, and says that she will remain at her father's, and threatens to "be angry"; but her wedded lord and master carries her off almost by main force; and, for the first time in her life, she learns in that mad journey to beg for "patience." Petruchio's wooing and his violence at the wedding are portrayed as making little or no change in Katherine's humor; but the cold and mud of the journey counteract her hot, dry choler, and start the cure.

In the country, moreover, she has broken with all the old associations of the luxurious town; and the severe regimen of cold and hunger and watching tempers her choleric spirit until she learns to "entreat." But even so, she is not yet fully cured, for, shamed by the presence of Hortensio, she declares: "My tongue will tell the anger of my heart"; but, on the return journey to her father's, the threats of Petruchio to give up the trip finally reduce her choler; and, to please her husband, she will even call the sun the moon, and address old Vincentio as a young girl—indeed, she even kisses her husband in the public street at his command. This "new-built virtue" not only wins the wager at the end of the comedy but even induces her grateful father to augment her dowry by twenty thousand crowns. She lectures the assembled company on the duties of a wife, and even forces the other wives to obey their husbands' orders. Despite Lucentio's fling in the last lines of the play, the cure seems to be complete; and, if Kate ever does come to dominate her husband and his household, it will be in the fashion of the Countess Olivia, by craft and not by violence.

The foregoing interpretation of Shakespeare's *Shrew* resolves several of the difficulties that have troubled critics in the play. It explains the unseemly behavior of a well brought-up young lady, and her father's reaction to that behavior. It presents Petruchio, not as a mere brute breaking his wife's will because she dares to cross him, but sympathetically, as Shakespeare clearly intended to present him: he is the worldly-wise physician-husband who has learned in his travels how to meet all occasions. His methods are severe, but at that they are more kindly than those of Coeffeteau, who would treat choleric persons quite in the fashion that violent lunatics were treated in that age. This interpretation of the play, moreover, suggests the function of the long "Induction," which some critics have considered quite extraneous. The comedy of the "Induction" centers on the cure of Sly's supposed fifteen years of "melancholy," a dangerous humor which like choler might lead to madness: thus these two humors have reduced both Kate and Sly to social uselessness; and both characters are shown as happily restored, to the joy of Sly's wife and of Kate's husband. Thus even the most boisterous scenes of the play are redeemed from mere crude farce; they have a meaning and a human interest with which one can sympathize. This psycho-medical background, moreover, is almost entirely Shakespeare's own addition to the stark old comedy from which he took his plot. The final cure justified the means; and, in the end, Petruchio has made Kate over into what she should have been, and she is no longer "Kate the Curst."

Shakespeare Constructs Two Interacting Worlds in *A Midsummer Night's Dream*

David Young

Because *A Midsummer Night's Dream* has four groups of characters without a single main character, the plot becomes a difficult tangle. David Young uses an analogy of geometric shapes to make it easier to follow. He identifies two worlds: the orderly world of Theseus and the confusing wilderness world of Oberon. The action flows through three spheres, from society to wilderness to improved society. Young identifies concentric worlds within the play and concentric circles of the characters' awareness of those worlds, from Bottom, in the center, who understands none, to the playwright, in the outer ring, who understands them all. With the devices of triangles, quadrangles, and circles, Young shows how the relationships change and the action proceeds during the course of the play. According to Young, the play achieves unity by means of a consistent tone and a final wedding scene. David Young is professor of English at Oberlin College, Oberlin, Ohio. He has published *The Heart's Forest: Shakespeare's Pastoral Plays* and a volume of poetry, *Sweating Out the Winter.*

There are two worlds in *A Midsummer Night's Dream*—the kingdom of Theseus and the kingdom of Oberon, the one an orderly society, the other a confusing wilderness. The action of the play moves between the two, as two groups of characters from the real and reasonable world find themselves temporarily lost in the imaginary and irrational world. This

From David Young, *Something of Great Constancy* (New Haven, CT: Yale University Press, 1966). Reprinted by permission of Yale University Press.

pattern of action corresponds closely both to the religious morality and the romance,[1] where the respective heroes often move on a narrative line that can be schematized as follows:

Morality:

$$\text{fall from grace} \;\Big/\; \begin{array}{c}\text{temporary}\\ \text{prosperity}\\ \text{of evil}\end{array} \;\Big/\; \begin{array}{c}\text{divine}\\ \text{reconciliation}\end{array}$$

Romance:
    separation / wandering / reunion

As the secular drama came to supersede the religious, it branched out, and one of the variations, based on the pastoral ideal, presented the movement through bad fortune to good fortune in spheres of action already familiar from the romance:

Pastoral Romance:
    society / wilderness / an improved society

The purest examples of this pattern in Shakespeare are *As You Like It* and the late romances, *Cymbeline, The Winter's Tale,* and *The Tempest,* but it may be found at work in plays as diverse as *Two Gentlemen* and *King Lear.*

ACTION FOLLOWS PATTERN OF TRADITIONAL PLAYS

In *A Midsummer Night's Dream* it is present at its most comic pitch: the danger which initially sends the central characters into the wilderness is less severe than in, say, *As You Like It,* and the corresponding need for some sort of social reform is slight. The wilderness, as a result, comes to play a more dominant role. In the pastoral romances, it is usually a pseudo-ideal and a temporary haven. In *A Midsummer Night's Dream,* as personified in the fairies, it governs most of the action and controls most of the characters, recalling the more powerful forces of disruption at work in the midsection of both morality and romance.

It will be noted that the spheres of action in these traditional narrative patterns do not alter significantly. It is the characters and, by imaginative extension, ourselves who alter as we move through the worlds in question, discovering their interaction. In *A Midsummer Night's Dream,* this process of discovery reveals that the opposing worlds seem to form concentric circles. At first, following the characters

1. medieval dramatic forms

from Athens to the woods, we may feel that the two areas are simply adjacent, but as Theseus and daylight reenter the play, we realize that it is possible to enter the woods and reemerge on the other side into human society. Thus, Theseus and his world seem to envelop the world of the woods. But Oberon and Titania, as we learn early in the play and are reminded directly at the end, are not the subjects of Theseus. Their awareness exceeds his, and their world is larger, enveloping his; he is their unconscious subject. Thus we discover another and larger circle, enclosing the first two. Then comes Puck's epilogue, which reminds us that everything we have been watching is a play, an event in a theater with ourselves as audience. Here is a still larger circle, envelop-

---

DIAGRAMS OF THE PLOT

David Young's geometric construction of the plot of A Midsummer Night's Dream *can be visualized with diagrams of the shapes he describes.*

Spheres of Action

ing all the others. The process stops there, but the discovery of ever more comprehensive circles inevitably suggests that there is another one still to be discovered. This is not merely a trick or a display of artistic ingenuity; treating us as it does to an expansion of consciousness and a series of epistemological discoveries,[2] it suggests that our knowledge of the world is less reliable than it seems.

CONCENTRIC CIRCLES OF AWARENESS

Thus it is that the concentric circles described above can also be used to depict the spectrum of awareness formed by the characters in the play. These are more usually depicted as levels on a kind of rising ladder of intelligence and consciousness, but the very action by which we learn of the dif-

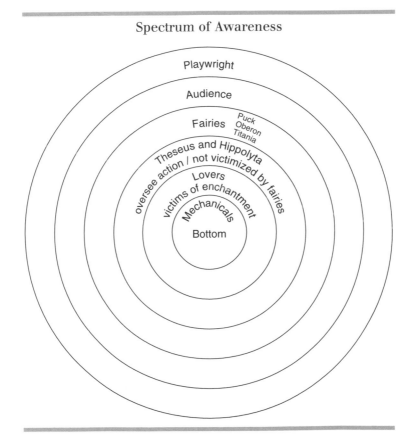

Spectrum of Awareness

Playwright

Audience

Fairies   Puck Oberon Titania

Theseus and Hippolyta

oversee action / not victimized by fairies

Lovers

victims of enchantment

Mechanicals

Bottom

2. relating to the nature of knowledge

ferences, that of one character standing aside to watch characters who are less aware of a given situation, suggests the enclosing image of a circle or sphere. In the inmost circle are the mechanicals, and at their center stands Bottom, supremely ignorant of all that is happening. All of the humor derived from Bottom depends on his absolute lack of awareness joined to the absolute confidence with which he moves through the play. If this makes him amusing, it also makes him sympathetic, as if we unconsciously recognized his kinship not only with the other characters but with ourselves. The difference, after all, is one of degree.

In the next circle belong the lovers; they are not much better off than the clowns, but the fact that they are largely victims of enchantment rather than native stupidity gives them claim to a fuller awareness, since Bottom's enchantment never alters his behavior or his nature. The circle beyond belongs to Theseus and Hippolyta, who oversee the action from a distance and are not victimized by the fairies. Hippolyta deserves the further station, on the basis of her con-

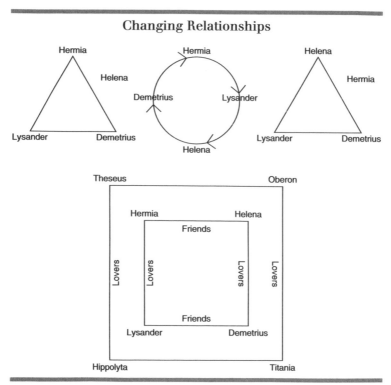

Changing Relationships

versation with Theseus at the beginning of the fifth act. The fairies occupy the next circle, Titania first, because she is tricked by her husband, then Oberon and Puck. Even these two, however, are not at all times fully aware of the course of events, and we, the audience, watch them as they watch the others. The furthest circle, then, belongs to us. Or is it the furthest? Does not the playwright belong still further out, overseeing not only the events of the play but our reaction to them, enchanting us as Puck enchants the lovers?

FOUR GROUPS OF CHARACTERS

The four groups into which the characters of *A Midsummer Night's Dream* fall present us with another spatial aspect of construction. The effect is like that of a fugue, in which we are simultaneously aware of several lines of movement and thus of position and interaction. Each of the four groups in the play has its own set of experiences. Since we know that these are occurring simultaneously, we are conscious of the location of each group and the ways in which the various actions impinge upon one another. This consciousness is essentially spatial; it requires harmonious resolution just as does the temporal action. If for no other reason, the fairies' entrance in the fifth act would be necessary as the final step in the series of group positionings. The other three groups have gathered there; the arrival of the fairies completes the choreography.

A large part of our interest in the comedy is directed to the way in which the four groups are handled. Their introduction, for example, is formal and at the same time intriguing enough to capture our interest as we gradually realize how the strands of action are to be divided. We meet each group in turn with whatever is necessary in the way of individual and group characterization as well as the details of exposition required to start each action. Theseus and Hippolyta begin the parade with their mood of revelry and a few key details about their wedding. Egeus bustles in, changing the tone and introducing the lovers' plot, with three of the four lovers present. The stage is then cleared for some conventional love dialogue, the plans which will initiate the action in the woods, and the introduction of the fourth lover. In the next scene, we meet the mechanicals and are treated to a full characterization of Bottom. The exposition prepares us for complications in the woods, but it also looks forward, as did that of Theseus, to the final events of the play. For the masque-like introduction of the fairy group, we shift to the second sphere of action. As the last details necessary to the exposition fall into place, Demetrius and Helena enter and the interwoven adventures of three of the groups begin, with Theseus and Hippolyta held in the background for the duration of the night.

It is clear by the time these four groups of characters have been introduced that we are witnessing an art that divides our attention among a number of subjects. The four groups are not unrelated. By the end of the exposition, all have been shown to have the royal wedding as a point of contact: it is the deadline set for Hermia by Theseus, the occasion for the clowns' performance, and the reason for the presence of the fairies. Other linkings and encounters will follow. Nonetheless, each group has a set of common characteristics and each will undergo a particular set of experiences.

The division of interest through multiplication of plots and characters is typical of Elizabethan drama, which has often been called an art of multiplicity. As Madeleine Doran has shown, it originated in medieval practices of narration and staging and continued to be valued in the Renaissance even by those critics who were theoretically committed to the unities. Those dramatists who practiced it risked chaos, since the traditional means of dramatic unification were not open to them. *A Midsummer Night's Dream* risks more than most. Not only does it avoid a single action, it has no central character to whom the various events are unmistakably related. Furthermore, it cannot even be said to have a single theme; its dispersal of interest among various groups and settings is a dispersal, in part, of subject matter as well. Yet Shakespeare achieves unity, partly through careful control of tone and setting and partly through his handling of the groups, a spatial organization which is almost geometrical in its order and which involves relationships within each group as well as among the four.

THE TRIANGLES AND QUADRANGLES OF RELATIONSHIPS

Our sense of the lovers' permutations,[3] for example, is distinctly spatial; almost any discussion of them is apt to resort to diagrammatic figures. We begin the play with a triangle,

___
3. complete changes or transformations

Lysander-Hermia-Demetrius, but we soon realize, as Helena's presence and importance is established, that it is in fact a quadrangle, with Helena the neglected corner. In the second act, Lysander's allegiance is suddenly switched, so that we have "cross-wooing," each man pursuing the wrong woman. We also have a circle, since each of the four parties is pursuing another: Hermia is looking for Lysander; he is wooing Helena; she continues to love Demetrius; and he is still enamored of Hermia. This is the quadrangle at its most disrupted state, and two steps are necessary to repair it. The first of these comes in the third act, when Demetrius is restored to Helena. This reverses the original triangle, and Hermia becomes the neglected party. The fourth act finds the quadrangle in its proper state, each man attached to the right woman, restoring a situation which predates the beginning of the play.

These permutations are further complicated by the question of friendship. Each member of the quadrangle has, potentially, one love and two friends therein, but the shifting of love relationships disrupts the friendships as well. Lysander and Hermia are at the outset alienated from Demetrius but friends of Helena, so much so that they tell her their secret. When Lysander falls in love with Helena, their friendship is of course destroyed; she thinks he is making fun of her. The next alteration, Demetrius' restoration to Helena, destroys the Hermia-Helena friendship: Hermia thinks Helena is somehow responsible; Helena thinks everyone is mocking her. Thus, the restoration of the proper love relationships also restores the friendships of all four; even Lysander and Demetrius, who were ready to fight to the death, are friends again at the end of the play.

The lovers' quadrangle is set within another calmer quadrangle involving the royal couples. We learn of its existence when Oberon and Titania meet. She immediately charges him with love of Hippolyta, "Your buskin'd mistress and your warrior love," and he counters:

> How canst thou thus, for shame, Titania,
> Glance at my credit with Hippolyta,
> Knowing I know thy love to Theseus?   (act 2, scene 1)

There are cross-purposes, it appears, within this group as well. They do not, however, lead to the complications that beset the lovers. Theseus and Hippolyta are unaware of the fairies' marital difficulties. Moreover, the true occasion of

the quarrel is the changeling boy,[4] so that Oberon's practic-
ing on Titania is all that is needed to restore the quadrangle
to harmony and enable the fairies to join forces for the ritual
blessing at the end.

Oberon solves his problems with Titania by finding her
an absurd lover, thus creating a sort of mock triangle with
Bottom as the oblivious third party. But Bottom is also a
lover in his role of Pyramus and is part of another absurd triangle in which he plays not the intruding beast, lion or ass,
but the rightful mate.

THE WEDDING BRINGS ALL GROUPS TOGETHER

These geometrical figures are of course illusory, but by use
of the analogy to which they point, we see more clearly the
constant interaction among the four character groups, the
collisions and entanglements which make their separate adventures interdependent. The lovers begin and end the play
with an attachment to the court of Theseus and the revels
surrounding his wedding. In between, they are the victims of
their journey to the woods and consequent involvement with
the fairies. The fairies, who have arrived to bless the royal
wedding, are finally able to arrange two more and to solve
their own difficulties through an involvement with the mechanicals. The mechanicals, intent on entertaining Theseus,
unwittingly entertain Oberon and Puck as well. Their involvement with the lovers is more subtle. It is true that their
entertainment finally has the four lovers as audience, but
Bottom's adventures, as well as the play he stars in, provide
a good deal of indirect comment on the lovers, most of it in
the form of parody. This kind of relationship belongs to
Shakespeare's practice of "mirroring.". . .

The discerning audience will finally find in the mirror of
the mechanicals' performance one more image—its own. . . .
If they should fail, they have only themselves to blame.
There is just a hint of mockery in Puck's epilogue:

> If we shadows have offended,
> Thinke but this, and all is mended—
> That you have but slumb'red here
> While these visions did appear.
> And this weak and idle theme,
> No more yielding but a dream.   (act 5, scene 1)

4. a child secretly exchanged for another

Anyone who is willing to admit that he has slept through this performance cannot claim to be very alert. In fact, he must inevitably be compared to those characters in the play who are willing to think that they have "dreamed" it, dismissing events which exposed them significantly. Shakespeare gives us our choice. We may remain within the outer circles of consciousness with Oberon, Puck, and himself, or we may doze off and fall inward toward the condition of Bottom and the lovers. In the mirror of *A Midsummer Night's Dream*, the spectator may find, even if he does not recognize, his very form and pressure.

Four Worlds Merge in *A Midsummer Night's Dream*

Madeleine Doran

Madeleine Doran describes the interaction of four sets of characters in A Midsummer Night's Dream. *These are: the court characters Theseus and Hippolyta, two pairs of lovers in the wood, Puck and the fairies, and the craftsmen rehearsing a play in the forest. All four groups, though separate at the beginning, interact within the play and come together for the marriage celebration at the end. Doran explains how Shakespeare uses prose, blank verse, and rhymed lines to set one group apart from the others and to create the appropriate tone for the actions of each group. Though* A Midsummer Night's Dream *may be less subtle artistically than* The Tempest, *Doran asserts that Shakespeare perfected this happy comedy. Madeleine Doran has taught English at Wellesley College, the University of Wisconsin at Madison, and Stanford University in California. She is the author of* Shakespeare's Dramatic Language *and* The Text of King Lear.

A Midsummer Night's Dream is one of Shakespeare's happiest comedies. It is called a dream because the improbable events of the story seem to the participants when they are over like something dreamed, true yet not true—such a dream of crossed loves, futile quarrels, and frustrated searches, of fairy spells and strange transformations as belongs to Midsummer Eve, June 23, a night when men are proverbially subject to fairy tricks and queer fancies. "Methought I was, and methought I had—But man is but a patched fool if he will offer to say what methought I had." Yet the play is not just a fairy tale, for everyone knows that love

Excerpted from *A Midsummer Night's Dream* by William Shakespeare, edited with an introduction by Madeleine Doran, The Pelican Shakespeare. Copyright © 1959, 1971 by Penguin Books, Inc. Copyright renewed, 1987 by Madeleine Kathryn Doran. Reprinted by permission of Penguin Books.

is blind, and that mortals possessed with it readily make delightful fools of themselves. The characters in the play are only visited with the midsummer madness common to lovers in or out of fairy-haunted woods.

The absurd dream, however, is followed by a "solemnity," a happy but serious celebration of a multiple wedding. Marriage, of course, is the expected ending of a comedy of love; but the formality of these nuptials and the presence of the fairies to sing an epithalamium[1] and to bless the bride-beds suggest that the play may have been written as an entertainment for a great wedding, just as Quince's play was written for the wedding festival of Theseus and Hippolyta. Attempts have been made to find such a wedding of a suitable date. . . .

The best indication of approximate date lies in the style. The blank verse shows the easy handling Shakespeare had attained after writing plays for six or seven years, without showing the bolder freedom and more complex rhythms of later years. Composition in 1594 or 1595 would make the play fall at the end of Shakespeare's first years of experiment with drama, during which time he learned to harness to the needs of a play his schoolboy training in rhetoric, his fondness for playing with words, metres, and rhymes, his delight in poetry for its own sake. Like *Richard II* and *Romeo and Juliet*, both probably to be dated about 1595, *A Midsummer Night's Dream* is full of lyricism, not subdued, yet fully controlled for a dramatic purpose. . . .

Setting and poetry are made to sustain and illuminate the action. So they are in *A Midsummer Night's Dream.* The poetry creates the wood, the moonlight, and the fairies, and it is in the wood, under fairy spells, that all the fantastic events of the night take place. . . .

The play is all of a piece, with its several actions, its fantasy and its low comedy, its variety of styles for different situations and characters, all contributing to the whole design.

FOUR GROUPS OF CHARACTERS

That design falls into four component groups of characters and their actions: Theseus and Hippolyta, whose court in Athens furnishes a frame setting for the main plot and whose expected wedding makes an occasion for the play; the four young lovers, who run away from Athens and whose

---

1. a lyrical poem in honor of a bride and bridegroom

misadventures in the wood make up the principal action (on the eve of May Day, by the way, rather than on the eve of Midsummer Night, as we might expect); the fairies in the wood, who are having troubles of their own, but who, more or less by the way, intervene in the lovers' affairs to make them first worse, then better; and the "hempen homespuns," a group of Athenian craftsmen who come into the wood to rehearse a little play they hope to present at court for the wedding festivities, and who, in an unexpected way, also fall foul of the fairies. The fairies also come to court at the end to bring their blessings to the three newly wedded couples. And so each of the plots and groups of characters touches one of the others at some point.

The court, where the action begins and ends, is elegant, ceremonious, a scene "with pomp, with triumph, and with revelling." The blank verse generally spoken there helps to set off the courtly background, with its greater formality and decorum, from the comic adventures of the lovers. Duke Theseus is slightly, but adequately, sketched as a hero, a huntsman, and a sage prince. He is a strong, sensible, kind ruler, not particularly imaginative, and skeptical of fantasy, whether in lovers' brains or in poets'. To make him so, in this play of all others, is a nice touch of Shakespearean irony. The court, for all its gaiety, is the stable world of common sense and social order.

LOVERS IN THE WOODS

The desperate alternatives Theseus lays before Hermia—either to marry Demetrius, the man of her father's choice, or to betake herself to a cloister—drive her and Lysander into the woods, with Demetrius hot after them and Helena close behind. This device of taking his characters away from court and city into a freer, half fairy-tale world (a device he was to employ again in *As You Like It, The Winter's Tale,* and *The Tempest*) Shakespeare first fully discovered in *A Midsummer Night's Dream.*

Credibility may be suspended for the sake of fun, of poetry, and of comic vision. By making the fairies responsible for the young men's change of heart, he plays lightly on his comic theme, that love is hardly a rational state; at the same time he saves his lovers from such harsh judgments of fickleness as readers are inclined to visit on Proteus in the earlier comedy of *The Two Gentlemen of Verona.* For one scarcely remembers, after such a night of errors, that Demetrius first altered his affections without the aid of the love-juice; his breach of faith seems like part of the dream. When the sick fancy is cured, the heart returns to its true-love. The plotting of the complications is neat. With Puck's applications of the juice and of its antidote, the young men's changes of heart follow a simple diagrammatic scheme: before the action of the play starts, each one loved his own girl; when it begins both love Hermia, then each loves the wrong girl, then both love Helena; finally, each loves the right girl again. As is fitting to such a state of things, neither lover can be much distinguished from the other, being both just infatuated young men, and as violently sure there was never anyone like Helena one minute as they had been sure the moment before there was never anyone like Hermia.

The girls have more personality and individuality. Hermia is little and dark and a spitfire; Helena is tall and blonde and weepy, making much of her feminine woes and helplessness, yet quite as dogged in pursuit of her man as Hermia. The verse of the lovers varies between the blank verse they speak with the court group or when showing some elevation of feeling (as in Helena's lovely lines on her childhood friendship with Hermia) and the pentameter couplets and cross-rhymes they speak when they are quarrelling or making love. These rhyming passages, with their slight artificiality and lightness of touch, heighten the comedy.

THE FAIRY WORLD

The third element in the play, the fairy world, furnishes a slight secondary plot, as well as the machinery for the confusion of the main plot. The family quarrel of Titania and Oberon over the changeling boy is invented, perhaps, simply to bring the love-juice into the play. But, characteristically, Shakespeare gives this minor action depth and atmosphere, with glimpses of an Indian princess on a faraway shore and of Theseus' abandoned loves, hence endowing it with a vitality of its own. The primary purpose of the magic herbs—one to blind the sight with fancied love, the other to cure it—appears, of course, to be to further Oberon's revenge on Titania.

But by his casual order to Puck to anoint the eyes of a disdainful youth in Athenian garments, the herbs are brought most naturally into the main plot, where Shakespeare uses them ingeniously both to tie and to untie the knot of his complication. The fairies appear to be very busy about mortal affairs, but their interventions are, on the whole, well intended. Though they are abroad at night, they are not powers of darkness. If their mischief or their spite sometimes brings vexations, their goodwill brings blessings. They are, in short, the minor powers of the unseen world that make the little things of daily life go right or wrong. Puck, besides, is the comic chorus of the play, its spirit of fun: "Lord, what fools these mortals be!" One would think he had had nothing to do with their foolishness.

PUCK AS ACTOR AND COMMENTATOR

Puck has two important functions in A Midsummer Night's Dream. *He magically carries out Oberon's commands, and he acts as a Greek chorus, commenting on situations. In act 3, scene 2, he puts juice on the sleeping Lysander's eyelids and declares that the lovers will be restored to their right partners.*

> On the ground
> Sleep sound.
> I'll apply
> To your eye,
> Gentle lover, remedy.
> [*Squeezes the herb on* LYSANDER'S *eyelids.*]
> When thou wak'st,
> Thou tak'st
> True delight
> In the sight
> Of thy former lady's eye;
> And the country proverb known,
> That every man should take his own,
> In your waking shall be shown:
> Jack shall have Jill;
> Naught shall go ill;
> The man shall have his mare again, and all shall be well.

Oberon and Titania, in their beauty, their rule over fairyland and a courtly train, their travelling of great distances, their powers of enchantment, and their limited influence over human affairs, are like "the Faery" of late medieval tales and ballads, known to everybody; sometimes, as well, of romances, which, extended and debased, had become the favorite popular reading of the sixteenth century. But Robin Goodfellow is a native country imp of folk superstition, a "puck," an ugly, merry, mischievous hobgoblin. His name "Goodfellow" is less a surname than a propitiatory epithet, for he has it in his power to annoy in the way that the modern gremlins have; but he is friendly enough if well treated. Left a bowl of milk on a tidy hearth, he will make the household chores go right; neglected, he will put everything at sixes and sevens. In associating "literary" with folk fairies Shakespeare was not doing anything novel or incongruous, for fairy lore in his day was already an inextricable mixture of literary tradition (both medieval and classical), folk belief, religious teaching (which associated the fairies with evil spirits), and poetic invention.

Like other poets before him, Shakespeare enriched the blend, and added something unusual; that is, the miniature size of the fairies, who were commonly not smaller than children and were often the size of adults. But since the parts of Shakespeare's fairies must have been taken on the stage by boys old enough to play them, their diminutiveness is mainly for poetic effect (as in Mercutio's Queen Mab speech in *Romeo and Juliet*), an imaginative suggestion of elegance and daintiness. It is the poetry, after all, which creates the enchantment of the wood. Titania and Oberon, in keeping with decorum, generally speak in blank verse, like the characters in the human court; their verse, too, carries the weight of the imaginative description of the fairy world. But Oberon's description of Titania's bower[2] and his instructions to Puck are given special emphasis by being rhymed; and his and Puck's spells are pronounced in verse of shorter metre, usually octosyllabic, or four-stress, lines rhyming alternately or in couplets. The little fairies sing in tripping measures with shorter lines.

BOTTOM AND THE MECHANICALS

The fourth element in the play, the group of "mechanicals," is brought into it for the salt of low comedy. But they, too, coming into the wood to rehearse their interlude, are led naturally into the action. Partly through the accident of their choosing a grassy plot near Titania's bower, partly through Puck's mischief, Bottom, with his "fair large ears," becomes the object of the dainty queen's deluded fancy. So the theme of love-blindness is played in another key, and given ludi-

2. a woman's private chamber

crous emphasis. Bottom's part, probably performed by Will Kempe, the famous comedian of Shakespeare's company, is in the same line of clowns as Launce in *The Two Gentlemen* and Dogberry in *Much Ado about Nothing.* Like Dogberry, Bottom is wonderfully self-sufficient. His aplomb is quite undisturbed by the refinements of Titania's court and by the love of the Fairy Queen. Bottom and his friends speak in prose, not primarily because of their social class, but in order to set off the tone of their comedy from the rest of the play. The courtiers speak in prose, too, when they are joking at the performance of the interlude.

That little play, which Bottom and his friends so much admire, is written partly in pentameter couplets, partly in a variation of the common ballad stanza. . . . The subject of the play, the story of Pyramus and Thisbe, was (like the story of Romeo and Juliet, its offshoot) a perennial tale of faithful and unfortunate love, and was well worn through centuries of retelling. The time and the scene of it, ancient Babylon, would seem fitting to the court of Theseus. . . .

This admixture, in *A Midsummer Night's Dream,* of romantic adventure, sympathetic sentiment, fantasy, burlesque, and earthy comedy, and of characters of high and low degree, was agreeable to English taste and to Shakespeare's genius. It was his first masterpiece in this kind of comedy that we call romantic, a kind he continued to develop and to vary for the rest of his life. Compared with the greater comedies to follow, richer in portrayal of character and deeper in sympathy, and compared especially with his other fairy-tale play, *The Tempest,* which is the product of his ripest wisdom and of his maturest art, *A Midsummer Night's Dream* may seem a pretty toy. But the lesser thing it does it does to perfection. It is a little triumph—one of the earliest of Shakespeare's plays in which things so disparate and so various are gathered up into a single whole.

A Midsummer Night's Dream as Entertainment for a Wedding

Paul N. Siegel

Since *A Midsummer Night's Dream* was, in all likelihood, written for a real Elizabethan wedding, Paul N. Siegel assumes modern readers and audiences may enjoy the play more if they imagine themselves as guests enjoying the marriage festivities. Siegel explains this complex set of perspectives: The guests see the royal couple Theseus and Hippolyta and, by association, the couple whose wedding they have come to celebrate. Since Theseus is a reasonable duke, he dismisses the dream creatures whose activities take place in the moonlight. But the guests witness the events of the lovers, fairies, and rehearsing mechanicals and get swept up by their world. Being intelligent guests, they are also aware that they are seeing an illusion, not reality.

Siegel then explains the play-within-a-play, the story of Pyramus and Thisbe, that to a degree resembles the story of Hermia and Lysander. It is to be entertainment for the wedding celebration of Theseus and Hippolyta as *A Midsummer Night's Dream* is entertainment for the wedding the guests are attending. In the final scene, the fairies arrive to bless the wedding, just as the guests have come to bless a wedding. When the fairies have ended their song, the bridal couple is left to themselves, and the wedding guests depart.

Paul N. Siegel has taught English at the University of Connecticut, the University of New York, and Ripon College and was professor of English at Long Island University. He has coedited Shakespearean studies, published *Shakespearean Tragedies and the Elizabethan Compromise,* and edited *His Infinite Variety: Major Shakespearean Criticism Since Johnson.*

Paul N. Siegel, "*A Midsummer Night's Dream* and the Wedding Guests," *Shakespeare Quarterly,* vol. 4 (1953). Reprinted by permission of the author and *Shakespeare Quarterly.*

The manner in which the marriage of Theseus and Hippolyta is made the setting of *A Midsummer Night's Dream*, the music, dancing and spectacle with which it is filled, and the virtual epithalamium[1] at the conclusion testify, it is generally agreed, that the play was written as part of the festivities of some aristocratic wedding. "Can anyone read the opening scene, or the closing speech of Theseus, and doubt that the occasion was a wedding?" ask the editors of the *New Cambridge Shakespeare;* and they add, "Be it remembered, moreover, how the fairies dominate the play; and how constantly and intimately fairies were associated with weddings by our Elizabethan ancestors, their genial favours invoked, their possible malign caprices prayed against." In the back of the minds of the wedding guests who composed the first audience of *A Midsummer Night's Dream* was at all times the awareness that the stage-performance which they were witnessing was a part of the wedding celebration in which they were engaged. Shakespeare, writing not only for all time but for the occasion, played upon this awareness, exploiting to the full the theatrical potentialities of a situation in which the audience saw on the stage an enactment of the circumstances in which it was at the same time participating in life. By reading the play with the occasion constantly in our minds, by becoming the wedding guests in our imagination, we can recapture something of the total aesthetic experience of its first-performance audience, an experience which adds to the experience of the audiences of all ages a teasing piquancy of its own.

"Now, fair Hippolyta," says Theseus in the first words of the play, which immediately set the background and tone, "our nuptial hour / Draws on apace." In rich, stately music he expresses to her his longing for the marriage night which is to come after four days and then turns to his master of revels and commands him to "stir up the Athenian youth to merriments" and "awake the pert and nimble spirit of mirth." For this wedding of the Duke of Athens is a public festivity to be celebrated "with pomp, with triumph, and with revelling." The wedding guests could not miss the flattering similarity between the Elizabethan bridal couple and the gracious, exalted pair of legendary antiquity. In the revels of this famous wedding they saw an historical analogy

1. a lyric ode in honor of a bride and bridegroom

with the revels of the present wedding, a feature of which was this very play, which was to stir them, the choicest of English aristocratic youth, to merriment.

No sooner are the words of Theseus spoken than Egeus, Hermia, Lysander and Demetrius come on the stage, as if in answer to the summons to merriment. The two pairs of lovers are like puppets in the hands of a puppet-master, now jerked this way, now that, now chasing after, now running away from, in an amusing exhibition of the vagaries of love and the absurdities to which it impels its victims. Their "fond pageant" is ideally suited for a wedding entertainment, for with what could a wedding play deal if not with love, and, since it must be written in the "pert and nimble spirit of mirth," how could love be presented if not as a pixilation which seizes young folk, from which they awake, as from a dream, to find themselves happy in their approaching marriage? Such must be the fate of the aristocratic young unmarried guests (although, to be sure, the happy consummation was dependent on their finding their true loves); such was the fate of their elders. While the love of ordinary aristocrats such as those who were on the stage and those who were viewing the play is thus presented sportively, the love of Theseus and Hippolyta, and by implication that of the august bridegroom and bride whose wedding was being celebrated, is decorously presented on a different level. About to be married, Theseus is free of the sighs, the silences, the variable humors of the lover of romance who has not yet won his mistress. His passion is controlled, his love dignified and elevated.

From his serene height Theseus looks down with humorous condescension and benevolent tolerance upon the lovers and their moon-struck madness. Finding them asleep in the woods (now entirely different in the early daylight from the moonlit grove in whose shadows the mischievous Puck had caused them to chase madly about) where he has come to hunt, he tells his huntsmen to wake them with their horns. It is as if this spectacle, in which what had been discord is resolved into harmonious concord, takes the place of the sound from afar of the baying of his hounds, their cries of varied pitch blending together, to which he had invited Hippolyta to listen: "We will, fair queen, up to the mountain's top / And mark the musical confusion / Of hounds and echo in conjunction."

At the sound of the horns the lovers open their eyes to a new world. The fantastic story they have to tell is regarded skeptically by Theseus.

> I never may believe
> These antique fables, nor these fairy toys.
> Lovers and madmen have such seething brains,
> Such shaping fantasies, that apprehend
> More than cool reason ever comprehends.
> The lunatic, the lover, and the poet
> Are of imagination all compact.   (act 5, scene 1)

Although an exalted figure, Theseus is an earthborn mortal and hence can only deem the lovers' story the product of their imaginations.

But the audience witnessing the play had seen the "fairy toys" whose existence he does not believe in, and it knew better. It knew that they were unseen powers in the lives of human beings in innumerable ways, crossing them, bemusing them, giving them good luck, and that disturbances in the fairy kingdom were reflected in disturbances in human affairs (although, to be sure, fairies being fairies and not gods or planets, these disturbances were nothing more serious than unusually bad weather). It knew that they looked with amusement upon the "fond pageant" of human beings working at cross-purposes, changing their minds, not knowing themselves and unaware of the fairy influences affecting their lives. It knew that great Theseus himself was under the special protection of the fairy queen and his fair bride under the protection of the fairy king.

But did it really know? How sure can one be, even though one has seen them, of the existence of beings so small that they can hide in an acorn and so elusively fleet that they can girdle the earth in forty minutes? Those fairy forms which had disappeared as Theseus' horns were heard sounding in the distance—were they real or a dream that the audience had shared with an ass? "I have had a dream, past the wit of man to say what dream it was. Man is but an ass, if he go about to expound this dream."

But although by the exercise of its imagination an audience may lose itself in a dramatic universe which a dramatist has created, it can never entirely forget, if it is beyond the most primitive level of response, that this dramatic universe is in fact a dramatic universe and not the world of reality—and the aristocratic wedding guests were not at all unsophisticated. As Theseus continued to speak of the imagination of the poet, he made them more sharply aware that this perplexing dream, this evanescent reality which they witnessed, was itself but part of a dramatic illusion.

As imagination bodies forth
The forms of things unknown, the poet's pen
Turns them to shapes and gives to airy nothing
A local habitation and a name.　　　　　　(act 5, scene 1)

The creatures of the fairy world, things unknown, had indeed been given shape, habitation ("a bank where the wild thyme blows, / Where oxlips and the nodding violet grows"); and names, names which Bottom had soon come to use with incongruous courtly familiarity ("Mounsieur Cobweb," "Mounsieur Mustardseed,") as he had addressed the members of the fairy court waiting upon him. And not only the creatures of the fairy world. Did not the speaker, Duke Theseus, himself have existence only in "antique fables," and was not the Duke Theseus before the audience but a poor player who passed his hour upon the stage and then was heard no more and who could as fittingly as Oberon be called a "king of shadows"? Some perception of this paradox must have made the keener members of Shakespeare's courtly audience sense an irony in the large assurance with which Theseus spoke of the lovers' story of "fairy toys" and of the fantasies of the poet, whose eye, "in a fine frenzy rolling, / Doth glance from heaven to earth, from earth to heaven." Perhaps, as Hippolyta replied, there was something to the lovers' story, after all. Perhaps—on a different level—it is true that the imaginative intuition of the poet can actually apprehend more essential truth than "cool reason," that there are more things in heaven and earth than the Duke dreamt of.

But "these things seem small and undistinguishable, / Like far-off mountains turned into clouds." When, as Hippolyta finished speaking, Lysander and Hermia, Demetrius and Helena came on the stage and Theseus broke off the discussion with the remark "Here come the lovers, full of joy and mirth," the wedding guests were brought back from such thoughts to the solid world of human society, of which marriage is the base. "Come now," they heard Theseus exclaim,

what masques, what dances shall we have,
To wear away this long age of three hours
Between our after-supper and bed-time?
Where is our usual manager of mirth?
What revels are in hand? Is there no play

> To ease the anguish of a torturing hour?   (act 5, scene 1)

The four days before the marriage ceremony was to be performed, to which he had referred at the beginning of the play, had passed, and the time was now close at hand. As the wedding guests realized this, they realized also that the play which they themselves were witnessing was, with the approach of the consummation of the marriage of its chief characters, coming to an end. Very likely this play too was a play of three hours between after-supper and bedtime, a presentation on a midsummer night which was the final part of the wedding revels. If so, the audience must have felt piqued at seeing the same situation duplicated upon the stage. With the enactment of the play which the stage-audience was watching, the time of the consummation of the stage-marriage and the time of the consummation of the actual marriage, which at first had been far apart, were becoming more and more closely synchronized: at the conclusion of the play-within-the-play the play itself would end, and both stage-marriage and actual marriage would be consummated. The perception of this and the fulfillment of the expectancy roused by the comical rehearsals of Bottom and his mates would have added relish to the wedding audience's enjoyment of the play-within-the-play as burlesque and would also have impressed on it the neatness of the play's conclusion.

THE PLAY-WITHIN-THE-PLAY

The play put on by the rude country artisans for the Duke, moreover, is not merely a burlesque of the performances put on by such groups during Elizabeth's progresses; it is a kind of comment on *A Midsummer Night's Dream* itself which gives added significance to the manner in which it completes it. The story of Pyramus and Thisbe of the play-within-the-play is, like that of *A Midsummer Night's Dream*, an illustration that "true lovers have been ever crossed" and that "the course of true love never did run smooth." Like Lysander and Hermia, Pyramus and Thisbe are forbidden by their parents to love. As with them, there is unfortunate misunderstanding and confusion, and Pyramus believes Thisbe to be dead, as for a time Hermia thought Lysander to have been slain by Demetrius. . . .

The play-within-the-play might be said to be a presentation in little of *A Midsummer Night's Dream* as it would be seen through a distorting medium. "This is the silliest stuff that ever I heard," says Hippolyta of it. The same might have been said of *A Midsummer Night's Dream* by a hardheaded businesslike man of affairs who would have no truck with fairies and such. In fact, it was said. "It is the most insipid ridiculous play that ever I saw in my life," wrote Mr. Samuel Pepys in his diary after having seen a Restoration performance of Shakespeare's airily fanciful comedy. Through the Pyramus-Thisbe play Shakespeare was subtly asking his aristocratic audience to regard his play with imaginative understanding and sympathy. "The best in this kind are but shadows," replies Theseus to Hippolyta, "and the worst are no worse if, imagination amend them." This is lordly graciousness, to which Shakespeare was appealing and which he was at the same time flattering: the aristocratic spectator would remedy in his own mind the defects of the piece being presented before him. "Our sport shall be to take what they mistake; / And what poor duty cannot do, noble respect / Takes it in might, not merit."

While asking his audience, however, to aid him with its imagination, Shakespeare was, with the assurance of genius, displaying his mastery of his art. Although the imaginative cooperation of an audience is necessary for the success of a play, the Pyramus-Thisbe scene shows that, despite the Duke's words of gracious condescension, not all of an audience's good will and tolerant receptivity can make rant moving. "This passion, and the death of a dear friend, would go near to make a man sad." The contrast between the crude literalism of a man with a lantern representing moonshine of the Pyramus-Thisbe scene and the poetic magic of the moon-drenched imagery of *A Midsummer Night's Dream* itself, between the inept explanatory comments that the play is but a play and not real life ("When lion rough in wildest rage doth roar, / Then know that I, as Snug the jointer, am / A lion fell") and the delicate suggestion that the play, while only reflecting life, may be a kind of enchanted mirror displaying unseen truths—this contrast is a daring virtuosity calling attention to itself at the close of its performance.

With the conclusion of the rustic dance that follows the artisans' play, the clock strikes, and the Duke announces: "The iron tongue of midnight hath told twelve. / Lovers, to bed; 'tis almost fairy time." Perhaps the actor who delivered these lines addressed himself to the bridal couple as well as to the two pairs of stage-lovers. At any rate, the wedding audience knew that the play was at an end and, if the play was indeed the conclusion of the revels, that it was time to go bedward.

FAIRIES ARRIVE TO BLESS THE WEDDING

But all was not yet over. As the Duke, his bride, and their court left, the torches illuminating the hall where the play was being performed were extinguished one after the other, and, with the chamber silent and, except for the flickering light from the hearth, dark, suddenly Puck appeared. For, as he proclaimed, now when "the wasted brands do glow," it was again time for the frolicsome fairies, "following darkness like a dream." After him came tripping Oberon, Titania and the members of the fairy court, taking the stage left vacant by the members of the Athenian court, with crowns of lighted tapers on their heads making them appear as dancing circles of light. They were here to bless the wedding of the noble pair under their protection, and, as they sang and danced, their song and dance, performed with fairy grace, contrasted with the rustic dance that had preceded it, masque following anti-masque, as was fit and proper. Their song, in which they were led by Oberon, is a song of benediction preliminary to their scattering through the great house to hallow all of its rooms and to bless it and its noble owners for all time:

> Now, until the break of day,
> Through this house each fairy stray.
> To the best bride-bed will we,
> Which by us shall blessed be;
> And the issue there create
> Ever shall be fortunate . . .
> With this field-dew consecrate,
> Every fairy take his gait,
> And each several chamber bless,
> Through this palace, with sweet peace;
> And the owner of it blest
> Ever shall in safety rest.
> Trip away; make no stay;
> Meet me all by break of day.   (act 5, scene 1)

And, as the fairies vanished from the stage with their "glimmering light," the wedding guests dispersed, leaving the bridal couple to themselves and the house to darkness—and, as the more imaginative ones may have half-believed, to the beneficent fairies.

CHAPTER 3

Shakespeare's Popular Romantic Comedies

READINGS ON
THE COMEDIES

As You Like It as Romance

Louis B. Wright and Virginia A. LaMar

Louis B. Wright and Virginia A. LaMar survey several elements that create romance and give *As You Like It* charm. The setting is the Forest of Arden, a countryside like the one of Shakespeare's youth. The theme is love in its many forms. Borrowing from the conventions of traditional romances, Shakespeare imbues his characters with spirit and life and never lets the absurdity of romantic comedy go too far. The authors cite Rosalind, Touchstone, and Jaques as the main contributors to humor and gentle satire. Wright and LaMar conclude that Shakespeare must have looked at love and liked what he saw. Until 1968, Louis B. Wright was director of the Folger Shakespeare Library in Washington, D.C., an institute that conducts and fosters research on Shakespeare and the Elizabethan period. Until 1968, Virginia A. LaMar was research assistant at and executive secretary of the Folger library. Both Wright and LaMar published books on Elizabethan England.

As You Like It appeals to the perennial love of the English-speaking peoples for the open country, for the glades and woods of a country perpetually green. On every holiday the towns and cities of England empty as the inhabitants stream outward in search of greenswards, meadows, parks, and forest paths. For the city dweller a touch of nature at Whitsuntide[1] or on August bank holiday means a return to quiet and sanity not to be found in the roar of cities. Shakespeare's Englishmen were as appreciative as their descendants of the countryside, and Shakespeare wrote into *As You Like It* his

1. the week beginning with Whitsunday, or Pentecost, the seventh Sunday after Easter

own poetic tribute to the attractions of the woodlands of Warwickshire. For the Forest of Arden, where he set the play, is Warwickshire, however many olive trees and lionesses the players might discover therein.

In the prose romances of chivalric adventure, the settings were usually in some unreal land of Arcady[2] where one found lovelorn maidens in the company of shepherds and shepherdesses. The forests most likely were inhabited by giants, dwarfs, hermits, and enchantresses, not to mention troublesome or strange fauna that included dragons, cockatrices,[3] and an occasional unicorn. Although Shakespeare took his story from a popular romance, he managed to domesticate his setting, and, as absurd as the plot is, one somehow feels that the scenery is not far from something he has seen and experienced. To the Londoner who saw the play at the Globe, it must have smelled of the woods to the north of the city on a May day.

The Theme and Plot

As Shakespeare sat in his London lodgings writing these swift-moving lines, his mind was far away in the woodlands north of the Avon, which bore the name of Arden. Scholars have learnedly argued that the setting is clearly in some French duchy and it must be in the Ardennes near the Flanders border. Whatever may be the nominal location, and whatever incongruities remain from the romance that was the source of the play, the atmosphere is that of the English countryside.

Shakespeare himself, like most Englishmen of the time, was not far removed from the country. Stratford-upon-Avon, then a country town of about two thousand people, nestles in one of the most beautiful counties of England, a well-watered land of forests, farms, and sheep pastures. The sheepcote[4] that Rosalind set out to buy could have been a stone's throw from Shakespeare's father's farm at Snitterfield. Shakespeare always displayed the common sense and balance that one frequently finds in men brought up in the country, and in *As You Like It* he exhibits in marked degree qualities that indicate a man in harmony with nature.

The theme of the play is love in various aspects, but Shakespeare never lets his treatment of the subject drift into ab-

2. a remote pastoral place   3. serpents that could kill with a glance   4. pen to hold sheep

surdity, as so often happened in the romances. He can laugh gaily and happily at the perplexities that love can bring, but he is neither sentimental nor cynical. Even Rosalind in love is able to display a sense of humor about love and lovers, including herself. In this play, Shakespeare is not concerned with profound overtones and cosmic truths. He is writing a play of merriment and good humor, and audiences have liked it from his day until our own.

THE FOREST OF ARDEN PARADISE

In act 2, scene 1, of As You Like It, *the exiled duke reaches the Forest of Arden and proclaims the virtues of its simple life over the perils of court life.*

DUKE S. Now, my co-mates and brothers in exile,
Hath not old custom made this life more sweet
Than that of painted pomp? Are not these woods
More free from peril than the envious court?
Here feel we but the penalty of Adam,
The seasons' difference; as, the icy fang
And churlish chiding[1] of the winter's wind,
Which, when it bites and blows upon my body
Even till I shrink with cold, I smile, and say
"This is no flattery; these are counselors
That feelingly[2] persuade me what I am."
Sweet are the uses of adversity,
Which, like the toad, ugly and venomous,
Wears yet[3] a precious jewel[4] in his head;
And this our life, exempt from public haunt,[5]
Finds tongues in trees, books in the running brooks,
Sermons in stones, and good in everything:
I would not change it.

1. scolding   2. earnestly, eagerly   3. nevertheless   4. brilliant eyes or toad-stone, believed a protection against poison   5. free from the masses of humans

Shakespeare derived the plot and most of the incidents in *As You Like It* from a prose romance, a short novel by Thomas Lodge entitled *Rosalynde, or Euphues' Golden Legacy* (1590). Lodge, writing in the elaborate and somewhat artificial "euphuistic" manner popular at the time, told his tale in a high and serious style without any humor. Fantastic romances were popular in the Elizabethan period and no one asked for verisimilitude.[5] Some of these romances, in cheap editions,

5. the appearance of truth or reality

delighted apprentices and others besides. Everyone knew about *Palmerin of England, Amadis of Gaul,* and a score of other chivalric romances of the kind that were the undoing of Cervantes' knight, Don Quixote. Like Cervantes, Shakespeare could utilize the themes of romance for gently satiric purposes, and in *As You Like It* he introduces characters that would have jarred in Lodge's story. Shakespeare's additions include the comic parts of Touchstone and Audrey, William, and Jaques. Someone has observed that Touchstone serves as a foil to Rosalind and the highborn characters in the play, as Sancho Panza provided homely humor to contrast with the high-flown notions of Don Quixote.

Although Shakespeare took over the absurd conventions of romance in plot and incident, he gave so much life and reality to his principal characters that his audience is willing to grant the illusions required of the plot. Readers of pastoral romances were accustomed to shepherds and shepherdesses wandering about rather aimlessly and penning sonnets to the objects of their affections. If these lovelorn folk encountered a dragon, a lion, or a unicorn, that was never surprising. If the villain met a saintly hermit and suddenly changed his way of life after a sermon from the holy man, that too was conventional and usual. It was never considered strange for maidens to go masquerading as pages or young warriors, and always disguises were so perfect that no father could tell his own daughter, nor a lover his own lady, though he might have spent the previous soliloquy mooning over the quality of her voice, the loveliness of her lips, or the color of her eyes. Such conventions Shakespeare took over part and parcel, but they do not trouble us any more than they troubled the author's contemporaries. We are concerned with other more compelling elements in *As You Like It.*

The modern reader or spectator still delights in the atmosphere of the play. He too smells the woods, the flowers, and the fresh fields of Arden or of whatever locality his imagination provides. It is a play for springtime and youth. Perhaps that is why it has been popular in schools and colleges for open-air performance.

THE CHARACTERS

The play is also filled with gaiety and humor of a quality that does not stale. Touchstone the fool is one of Shakespeare's most amusing comic characters and one that has given scope to many stage comedians. The first actor to play this part was Shakespeare's colleague Robert Armin, and Shakespeare obviously wrote the part for him. Armin had succeeded Will Kemp, the previous actor of clowning roles in Shakespeare's company, and some stage historians have seen a shift in the quality of the clowns with this change. The later fools or clowns are more intellectualized and wittier than the parts played by Kemp, who himself was famous for buffoonery and slapstick comedy.

Touchstone serves as a sort of chorus or a commentator on the action and the behavior of the other characters. When conversation becomes too lofty, especially when the sentiments of the lovers begin to soar away into metaphor, it is Touchstone who brings the tone down to earth with his homespun comments. When others talk of ethereal love, he exemplifies the physical desires felt by ordinary folk. He recognizes that "wedlock would be nibbling," and he remarks to Audrey: "Come, sweet Audrey./ We must be married, or we must live in bawdry."

Rosalind is typical of the heroines of pastoral romance only in external appearance, because her manner is too genuine and lifelike for the usual romance. Though she is madly in love with Orlando, she can play a practical joke upon him and make witty jests about lovers, a trait not characteristic of the weepy maidens in most of the prose tales. Not one of them, even masquerading as some other character, would have said, as Rosalind commented, that "Men have died from time to time, and worms have eaten them, but not for love." Rosalind is one of Shakespeare's most attractive women—witty, frank, generous, and courageous. The role has been a favorite with many of the most attractive actresses of the past century and a half.

Shakespeare exhibits assurance, ease, and originality in *As You Like It.* He was a successful playwright and he was conscious of his own ability to handle the theme with professional skill. But the play represents more than a new height of professional competence. It shows an adjustment to the world in which the author lived and a wholesome delight in the universe around him. Although critics have speculated on the significance of the melancholy Jaques and the possible reflection in his commentary of personal attitudes of the author, such speculation is beside the point. Jaques is of a type fashionable on the stage at that moment. Although he is not the typical malcontent whose cynicism was a popular theatrical convention in the last decade of the sixteenth century, he does represent a rather conventional type that affected a melancholy and dyspeptic[6] attitude toward the world. As such he was amusing to the audiences of the time, but from the happy tone of the play there is no suggestion that Shakespeare meant Jaques to speak the author's own sentiments. Indeed, the spirit of the play is that of wholesome satisfaction with a world that is essentially good. Even the usurping Duke in the end undergoes a conversion and surrenders his lands to the rightful owner, and it is significant that Shakespeare is too charitable to have him killed in battle as Lodge had done in his novel.

In *As You Like It* Shakespeare studied the effects of love as it manifested itself in a variety of individuals: spirited and highborn Rosalind; brave and desperate Orlando; earthy Touchstone, content for a time with Audrey, "an ill-favored thing . . . but mine own"; selfish and thoughtless Phebe; faithful and loyal Silvius; and all the rest who are touched with an emotion universal in its influence upon men and women. Nowhere in the play does the treatment of this theme suggest anything but a healthy attitude. Shakespeare had looked on love and been content with what he found.

6. morose and cranky, as if suffering from indigestion

As You Like It: A Comedy of Discovery

Helen Gardner

Helen Gardner says that in *As You Like It* Shake-speare's characters discover happiness by recogniz-ing and accepting the briars with the roses, the sour with the sweet. This theme develops, Gardner ar-gues, through Shakespeare's setting, plot, and char-acterization. The Forest of Arden is a welcome refuge from the cruelties of court life, but it is a cold place touched with sorrows. In a plot built on dis-guises and trial and error, characters develop an un-derstanding of reality and human imperfection. Moreover, Shakespeare has paired characters to illu-minate the contrasts in the debate between court and forest, between happiness and cynicism. Though the debate is carried out in the actions of many charac-ters, Touchstone and Jaques most directly articulate opposing views of life. The end of the play, according to Gardner, is a graceful pageant in which everyone is content. Even Jaques is happy in his singular cyni-cism. Helen Gardner was a fellow of St. Hilda's Col-lege, Oxford. She has published *The Art of T.S. Eliot*, *The Divine Poems of Donne*, and *The Business of Crit-icism*, as well as numerous essays and articles.

As its title declares, this is a play to please all tastes. . . . For the simple, it provides the stock ingredients of romance: a handsome, well-mannered young hero, the youngest of three brothers, two disguised princesses to be wooed and wed, and a banished, virtuous Duke to be restored to his rightful throne. For the more sophisticated, it propounds, in the manner of the old courtly literary form of the *débat*, a question which is left to us to answer. . . .

In *As You Like It* the plot is handled in the most perfunctory way. Shakespeare crams his first act with incident in order to get everyone to the forest as soon as he possibly can and, when he is ready, he ends it all as quickly as possible. A few lines dispose of Duke Frederick, and leave the road back to his throne empty for Duke Senior. As for the other victim of a wicked brother, it is far more important that Orlando should marry Rosalind than that he should be restored to his rights.

Mrs. Suzanne Langer, in her brilliant and suggestive book *Feeling and Form*, has called comedy an image of life triumphing over chance. She declares that the essence of comedy is that it embodies in symbolic form our sense of happiness in feeling that we can meet and master the changes and chances of life as it confronts us.... The great symbol of pure comedy is marriage by which the world is renewed, and its endings are always instinct with a sense of fresh beginnings. Its rhythm is the rhythm of the life of mankind, which goes on and renews itself as the life of nature does....

THE COMEDY SET IN THE FOREST OF ARDEN

In *As You Like It* Shakespeare returned to the pattern of *A Midsummer-Night's Dream*, beginning his play in sorrow and ending it with joy, and making his place of comic encounters a place set apart from the ordinary world. The Forest of Arden ranks with the wood near Athens and Prospero's island[1] as a place set apart, even though, unlike them, it is not ruled by magic. It is set over against the envious court ruled by a tyrant, and a home which is no home because it-harbors hatred, not love.... But, of course, it is no such Elysium. It contains some unamiable characters. Corin's master is churlish and Sir Oliver Martext is hardly sweet-natured; William is a dolt and Audrey graceless. Its weather, too, is by no means always sunny. It has a bitter winter. To Orlando, famished with hunger and supporting the fainting Adam, it is "an uncouth forest" and a desert where the air is bleak. He is astonished to find civility among men who

in this desert inaccessible,
Under the shade of melancholy boughs,
Lose and neglect the creeping hours of time.

In fact Arden does not seem very attractive at first sight to

1. *A Midsummer Night's Dream* is set in a wood and *The Tempest* on an island.

the weary escapers from the tyranny of the world. Rosalind's "Well, this is the forest of Arden" does not suggest any very great enthusiasm; and to Touchstone's "Ay, now I am in Arden; the more fool I: when I was at home, I was in a better place: but travellers must be content," she can only reply "Ay, be so, good Touchstone." It is as if they all have to wake up after a good night's rest to find what a pleasant place they have come to. Arden is not a place for the young only. Silvius, for ever young and for ever loving, is balanced by Corin, the old shepherd, who reminds us of that other "penalty of Adam" beside "the seasons' difference": that man must labor to get himself food and clothing. Still, the labor is pleasant and a source of pride: "I am a true laborer: I earn that I eat, get that I wear, owe no man hate, envy no man's happiness, glad of other men's good, content with my harm; and the greatest of my pride is to see my ewes graze and my lambs suck."

Arden is not a place where the laws of nature are abrogated and roses are without their thorns. If, in the world, Duke Frederick has usurped on Duke Senior, Duke Senior is aware that he has in his turn usurped upon the deer, the native burghers of the forest. If man does not slay and kill man, he kills the poor beasts. Life preys on life. Jaques, who can suck melancholy out of anything, points to the callousness that runs through nature itself as a mirror of the callousness of men. The herd abandons the wounded deer, as prosperous citizens pass with disdain the poor bankrupt, the failure. The race is to the swift. But this is Jaques's view. Orlando, demanding help for Adam, finds another image from nature:

> Then but forbear your food a little while,
> Whiles, like a doe, I go to find my fawn
> And give it food. There is a poor old man,
> Who after me hath many a weary step
> Limp'd in pure love: till he be first suffic'd,
> Oppress'd with two weak evils, age and hunger,
> I will not touch a bit.

ARDEN BLENDS THE SWEET AND THE SOUR

. . . It is in Arden that Jaques presents his joyless picture of human life, passing from futility to futility and culminating in the nothingness of senility—"sans everything"; and in Arden also a bitter judgment on human relations is lightly passed in the twice repeated "Most friendship is feigning, most loving mere folly." But then one must add that hard on the heels of Jaques's melancholy conclusion Orlando enters with Adam in his arms, who, although he may be "sans teeth" and at the end of his usefulness as a servant, has, beside his store of virtue and his peace of conscience, the love of his master. . . .

THE SEVEN AGES OF MAN

In act 2, scene 7 of As You Like It, *Jaques explains how he sees humans move through seven ages as players on the stage of life.*

> All the world's a stage,
> And all the men and women merely players.
> They have their exits and their entrances,
> And one man in his time plays many parts,
> His acts being seven ages. At first, the infant,
> Mewling and puking in the nurse's arms.
> Then the whining schoolboy, with his satchel
> And shining morning face, creeping like snail
> Unwillingly to school. And then the lover,
> Sighing like furnace, with a woeful ballad
> Made to his mistress' eyebrow. Then a soldier
> Full of strange oaths and bearded like the pard,
> Jealous in honour, sudden and quick in quarrel,
> Seeking the bubble reputation
> Even in the cannon's mouth. And then the justice,
> In fair round belly with good capon lin'd,
> With eyes severe and beard of formal cut,
> Full of wise saws and modern instances;
> And so he plays his part. The sixth age shifts
> Into the lean and slipper'd pantaloon,
> With spectacles on nose and pouch on side;
> His youthful hose, well sav'd, a world too wide
> For his shrunk shank, and his big manly voice,
> Turning again toward childish treble, pipes
> And whistles in his sound. Last scene of all,
> That ends this strange eventful history,
> Is second childishness and mere oblivion,
> Sans teeth, sans eyes, sans taste, sans everything.

The whole play is a balance of sweet against sour, of the cynical against the idealistic, and life is shown as a mingling of hard fortune and good hap. The lords who have "turned ass," "leaving their wealth and ease a stubborn will to please," are happy in their gross folly, as Orlando is in a lovesickness which he does not wish to be cured of. What Jaques has left out of his picture of man's strange eventful pilgrimage is love and companionship, sweet society, the banquet under the boughs to which Duke Senior welcomes Orlando and Adam. Although life in Arden is not wholly idyllic, and this place set apart from the world is yet touched by the world's sorrows and can be mocked at by the worldly wise, the image of life which the forest presents is irradiated by the conviction that the gay and the gentle can endure the rubs of fortune and that this earth is a place where men can find happiness in themselves and in others.

The Forest of Arden is, as has often been pointed out, a place which all the exiles from the court, except one, are only too ready to leave at the close.... The stately masque of Hymen marks the end of this interlude in the greenwood, and announces the return to a court purged of envy and baseness.

ARDEN IS A PLACE OF DISCOVERY

Like other comic places, Arden is a place of discovery where the truth becomes clear and where each man finds himself and his true way. This discovery of truth in comedy is made through errors and mistakings. The trial and error by which we come to knowledge of ourselves and of our world is symbolized by the disguisings which are a recurrent element in all comedy, but are particularly common in Shakespeare's. Things have, as it were, to become worse before they become better, more confused and farther from the proper pattern. By misunderstandings men come to understand, and by lies and feignings they discover truth.

If Rosalind, the princess, had attempted to "cure" her lover Orlando, she might have succeeded. As Ganymede, playing Rosalind, she can try him to the limit in perfect safety, and discover that she cannot mock or flout him out of his "mad humor of love to a living humor of madness," and drive him "to forswear the full stream of the world, and to live in a nook merely monastic." By playing with him in the disguise of a boy, she discovers when she can play no more. By love of a shadow, the mere image of a charming youth, Phoebe discovers that it is better to love than to be loved and scorn one's lover. This discovery of truth by feigning, and of what is wisdom and what folly by debate, is the center of *As You Like It.*

It is a play of meetings and encounters, of conversations

and sets of wit: Orlando versus Jaques, Touchstone versus Corin, Rosalind versus Jaques, Rosalind versus Phoebe, and above all Rosalind versus Orlando. The truth discovered is, at one level, a very "earthy truth": Benedick's discovery that "the world must be peopled." The honest toil of Corin, the wise man of the forest, is mocked at by Touchstone as "simple sin." He brings "the ewes and the rams together" and gets his living "by the copulation of cattle." The goddess Fortune seems similarly occupied in this play: "As the ox hath his bow, the horse his curb, and the falcon her bells, so man hath his desires; and as pigeons bill, so wedlock would be nibbling." Fortune acts the role of a kindly bawd. Touchstone's marriage to Audrey is a mere coupling. Rosalind's advice to Phoebe is brutally frank: "Sell when you can, you are not for all markets." The words she uses to describe Oliver and Celia "in the very wrath of love" are hardly delicate, and after her first meeting with Orlando she confesses to her cousin that her sighs are for her "child's father." Against the natural background of the life of the forest there can be no pretence that the love of men and women can "forget the He and She."

But Rosalind's behavior is at variance with her bold words. Orlando has to prove that he truly is, as he seems at first, the right husband for her, and show himself gentle, courteous, generous and brave, and a match for her in wit, though a poor poet. In this, the great coupling of the play, there is a marriage of true minds. The other couplings run the gamut downwards from it, until we reach Touchstone's image of "a she-lamb of a twelvemonth" and "a crooked-pated, old, cuckoldy ram," right at the bottom of the scale. As for the debate as to where happiness is to be found, the conclusion come to is again, like all wisdom, not very startling or original: that "minds innocent and quiet" can find happiness in court or country:

> Happy is your Grace,
> That can translate the stubbornness of fortune
> Into so quiet and so sweet a style.

And, on the contrary, those who wish to can "suck melancholy" out of anything, "as a weasel sucks eggs."

JAQUES AND TOUCHSTONE ARE CONTRASTED

In the pairing one figure is left out. "I am for other than for dancing measures," says Jaques. Leaving the hateful sight of revelling and pastime, he betakes himself to the Duke's abandoned cave, on his way to the house of penitents where Duke Frederick has gone. The two commentators of the play are nicely contrasted. Touchstone is the parodist, Jaques the cynic. . . .

In everything that Touchstone says and does gusto, high spirits, and a zest for life ring out. Essentially comic, he can adapt himself to any situation in which he may find himself. Never at a loss, he is life's master. The essence of clowning is adaptability and improvisation. The clown is never baffled and is marked by his ability to place himself at once *en rapport* with his audience, to be all things to all men, to perform the part which is required at the moment. Touchstone sustains many different roles. . . . It is right that he should parody the rest of the cast, and join the procession into Noah's ark with his Audrey.

Jaques is his opposite. He is the cynic, the person who prefers the pleasures of superiority, cold-eyed and cold-hearted. The tyrannical Duke Frederick and the cruel Oliver can be converted; but not Jaques. He likes himself as he is. He does not wish to plunge into the stream, but prefers to stand on the bank and "fish for fancies as they pass." Sir Thomas Elyot said that dancing was an image of matrimony: "In every daunse, of a most auncient custome, there daunseth together a man and a woman, holding eche other by the hande or the arme, which betokeneth concorde." There are some who will not dance, however much they are piped to, any more than they will weep when there is mourning. "In this theatre of man's life," wrote Bacon, "it is reserved only for God and angels to be lookers on." Jaques arrogates to himself the divine role. He has opted out from the human condition.

JAQUES GIVES EXPRESSION TO SAD REALITY

It is characteristic of Shakespeare's comedies to include an element that is irreconcilable, which strikes a lightly discordant note, casts a slight shadow, and by its presence questions the completeness of the comic vision of life. . . .

It is characteristic of the delicacy of temper of *As You Like It* that its solitary figure, its outsider, Jaques, does nothing whatever to harm anyone, and is perfectly satisfied with himself and happy in his melancholy. Even more, his melancholy is a source of pleasure and amusement to others. The Duke treats him as virtually a court entertainer, and he is a natural butt for Orlando and Rosalind. Anyone in the play can put him down and feel the better for doing so. All the same his presence casts a faint shadow. His criticism of the world has its sting drawn very early by the Duke's rebuke to him as a former libertine, discharging his filth upon the world, and he is to some extent discredited before he opens his mouth by the unpleasant implication of his name. But he cannot be wholly dismissed. A certain sour distaste for life is voided through him, something most of us feel at some time or other. If he were not there to give expression to it, we might be tempted to find the picture of life in the forest too sweet. His only action is to interfere in the marriage of Touchstone and Audrey; and this he merely postpones. His effect, whenever he appears, is to deflate: the effect does not last and cheerfulness soon breaks in again. Yet as there is a scale of love, so there is a scale of sadness in the play. It runs down from the Duke's compassionate words:

> Thou seest we are not all alone unhappy:
> This wide and universal theatre
> Presents more woeful pageants than the scene
> Wherein we play in,

through Rosalind's complaint "O, how full of briers is this working-day world," to Jaques's studied refusal to find anything worthy of admiration or love. . . .

The appearance of the god to present daughter to father and to bless the brides and grooms turns the close into a solemnity, an image of the concord which reigns in Heaven and which Heaven blesses on earth. But this, like much else in the play, may be taken as you like it. There is no need to see any more in the god's appearance with the brides than a piece of pageantry which concludes the action with a graceful spectacle and sends the audience home contented with a very pretty play.

Creative Devices Make *Twelfth Night* a Great Comedy

Harold Jenkins

Harold Jenkins argues that Shakespeare makes *Twelfth Night* his greatest romantic comedy by using traditional devices in creative ways. Jenkins says Orsino, for example, is more imaginative than the traditional devoted romantic lover. Jenkins identifies Shakespeare's metaphor of music as the food of love, suggesting that the spirit of love is as transitory as music. Romantic comedies frequently employ devices such as a message sent by letter, the request for a picture, and the gift of a ring; Jenkins explains how Shakespeare effectively modifies these devices. Finally, according to Jenkins, with the subplot involving Olivia's steward Malvolio, Shakespeare creates a contrast that heightens Olivia's transformation and the golden time that comes to Orsino and Olivia. Harold Jenkins has been professor of English literature at Westfield College, London. He is the author of *Henry Chettle* and *Edward Benlowes* and the joint editor of the Arden Shakespeare edition.

Now if *Twelfth Night* is the greatest of Shakespeare's romantic comedies, it is partly because of its success in embodying these feelings of wonder in the principal persons of the play. Stories of romantic love owe something of their perennial appeal, we need not be ashamed to admit, to the taste for tales of pursuit and mysterious adventure, as well as to what psychologists no doubt explain as the sublimation of the natural impulses of sex. But the devotion which the romantic lover bestows upon a woman as pure as she is unattainable may also symbolize the mind's aspiration towards some ever alluring but ever elusive ideal. . . .

Excerpted from Harold Jenkins, *Shakespeare's "Twelfth Night,"* Rice Institute Pamphlet XLV (1959). Reprinted by permission of Rice University.

But a still subtler situation may arise with characters who are from the beginning full of devotion to an ideal of love while mistaking the direction in which it should be sought. This, I take it, is the case with Orsino and Olivia. Orsino, with whom *Twelfth Night* begins and who draws us from the start into the aura of his imagination, is in some ways the most perfect of Shakespeare's romantic lovers simply because he is so much more. . . .

ORSINO: THE ROMANTIC LOVER

Orsino, instead of a servant who laughs at him for loving, has a page who can show him how to do it. "If I did love you in my master's flame," says Cesario, I would

> Make me a willow-cabin at your gate
> And call upon my soul within the house

till all the hills reverberated with the name of the beloved. This famous willow-cabin speech, often praised for its lyricism, is of course no less a parody of romantic love. . . . But the parody, though it has its hint of laughter, is of the kind that does not belittle but transfigures its original. So it comes as no surprise when Olivia, hitherto heedless of sighs and groans, suddenly starts to listen. To the page she says, "*You* might do much," and these words are her first acknowledgement of love's power. Orsino, content to woo by proxy a woman who immures herself in a seven-year mourning for a dead brother, may have the glamor of a knight of romance but he is *not* quite free from the risk of absurdity. He seems, they tell us with some justice, in love not so much with a woman as with his own idea of love. But what they do not so often tell us is how splendid an idea this is. . . . They[1] were said, it will have been noticed, to *thunder,* and his sighs were *fire.* If he indulges his own emotions, this is in no mere dilettantism but with the avidity of hunger.

> If music be the *food* of love, play on,
> give me *excess* of it, that *surfeiting,*
> The *appetite* may sicken and so die. [emphasis added]

This wonderful opening speech suggests no doubt the changeableness of human emotion. "Play on . . . that strain again! It had a dying fall. . . . Enough, no more! 'Tis not so sweet now as it was before." But if the spirit of love is as transitory as music and as unstable as the sea, it is also as living

---

1. his groans for love

and capacious. New waves form as often as waves break; the shapes of fancy, insubstantial as they are, make a splendor in the mind, and renew themselves as quickly as they fade. So Orsino's repeated rejections by his mistress do not throw him into despair. Instead he recognizes, in her equally fantastic devotion, a nature of surpassingly "fine frame" and he reflects on how she *will* love when the throne of her heart shall find its "king." How too will *he* love, we are entitled to infer, when his inexhaustible but as yet deluded fancy shall also find the true sovereign it seeks. This of course it does at the end of the play when he exchanges all his dreams of passion for the love of someone he has come to know. . . .

VIOLA: DISGUISED BUT GENUINE

Orsino is still sending messages to one he calls his "sovereign," but *his* throne, we may say, is still unoccupied. For his splendid fantasies are as yet self-regarding. When Viola objects, "But if she cannot love you, sir?" he dismisses this with "I cannot be so answered." Yet when she simply retorts, "Sooth, but you must," he receives his first instruction in the necessity of accommodating his fantasies to practical realities. And soon he begins, however unwittingly, to learn. As Viola tells the history of her father's daughter, though he does not see that she is speaking of herself, he finds himself for the first time giving attention to a sorrow not his own. "But died thy sister of her love, my boy?" he asks. To this Viola can only reply, "I know not"; for at this stage in the drama the issue is still in the balance, though Orsino's new absorption in another's plight will provide us with a clue to the outcome. In the very act of sending a fresh embassy to his mistress his thoughts are momentarily distracted from his own affair. When it is necessary for Viola to prompt him— "Sir, shall I to this lady?"—though he rapidly collects himself, we know that his development has begun.

In the emotional pattern of the play Viola represents a genuineness of feeling against which the illusory can be measured. As the go-between she is of course also at the center of the plot. It is her role to draw Orsino and Olivia from their insubstantial passions and win them to reality. But her impact upon each of them is inevitably different. Orsino, whom she loves but cannot tell her love, responds to her womanly constancy and sentiment; Olivia, whom she cannot love but has to woo, is to be fascinated by her page-boy effrontery and wit.

THE ENCOUNTER OF OLIVIA AND THE PAGE

Now in all the stories of the woman-page who woos for her master and supplants him, the transference of the mistress's affections must be the pivot of the action.... In *Twelfth Night* he[2] takes care to throw the emphasis upon it from the first. Viola is got into her page-boy clothes before we are halfway through the first act. The plausibility of this, notwithstanding Mrs. Lennox and Dr. Johnson, is not the question. What matters is that the encounter of the lady and the page, upon which the plot is to turn, shall be momentous. ...

THE CLOWN'S SONG

In Twelfth Night, *the clown Feste sings on request. In act 2, scene 3, Sir Toby Belch and Sir Andrew Aguecheek call for a love song, which Feste then sings.*

SIR AND. Excellent! Why, this is the best fooling, when all is done. Now, a song.

SIR TO. Come on, there is sixpence for you—let's have a song.

SIR AND. There's a testril[1] of me too. If one knight give a—

CLO. Would you have a love song, or a song of good life?

SIR TO. A love song, a love song.

SIR AND. Aye, aye. I care not for good life.

CLO. [*Sings.*]

O mistress mine, where are you roaming?
Oh, stay and hear, your truelove's coming,
    That can sing both high and low.
Trip no further, pretty sweeting,
Journeys end in lovers meeting,
    Every wise man's son doth know.

SIR AND. Excellent good, i' faith.

SIR TO. Good, good.

CLO. [*Sings.*]

What is love? 'Tis not hereafter,
Present mirth hath present laughter,
    What's to come is still unsure.
In delay there lies no plenty,
Then come kiss me, sweet and twenty,[2]
    Youth's a stuff will not endure.

1. coin worth sixpence   2. a happy, sweet girl

2. Shakespeare

By now the page is at the gate. Indeed three different messengers announce him. Sir Toby of the weak pia mater is too drunk to do more than keep us in suspense, but Malvolio precisely catalogues the young man's strange behavior, till we are as curious to see him as is Olivia herself. "Tell him he shall not speak with me," she has insisted; but when this changes to "Let him approach," the first of her defences is down. Our interest in each of them is now at such a height that the moment of their meeting cannot fail to be electric.... However, Cesario only pretends not to recognize Olivia so as to confound her with his raillery. "Most radiant, exquisite and unmatchable beauty," he begins and then breaks off to enquire whether the lady before him is the radiant unmatchable or not. As he has never seen her, how can he possibly tell?...

TRADITIONAL DEVICES: LETTER, PICTURE, AND RING

In *Twelfth Night* the letter, the picture, and the ring are changed almost out of recognition. Shakespeare's superbly original invention allows Orsino to dispense with them; yet they are all vestigially[3] present. Instead of bearing missives, the page is given the task of acting out his master's woes, and so instead of the lover's own letter we are to have the page's speech. This cunningly diverts attention from the message to the messenger, and the effect is still further enhanced when even the speech never gets delivered apart from its opening words. Instead there is talk about the speech—how "excellently well penn'd," how "poetical" it is—and are you really the right lady so that I may not waste the praise I have taken such pains to compose? Olivia in turn delights us by matching Cesario's mockery, but as we watch them finesse about how and even whether the speech shall be delivered, their mocking dialogue says more than any formal speech could say. In fact the very circumventing of the speech brings them to the heart of its forbidden theme.

And so we come to the picture. There is of course no picture, any more than there was a letter; but the convention whereby the lover asks for a picture of his mistress is made to provide a metaphor through which the witty duel may proceed. Olivia draws back the curtain and reveals a picture, they talk of the colors that the artist's "cunning hand laid on,"

---

3. constituting a trace or remnant

and Cesario asks for a copy. But the curtain Olivia draws back is her own veil, the artist is Nature, and the copy of Nature's handiwork will come as the fruit of marriage. Again the suggestion that Olivia could have a child. The cloistress who dedicates herself to the dead is reminded of the claims of life. She waves them aside for the moment by deftly changing the application of the metaphor. Certainly there shall be a copy of her beauty; why not an inventory of its items? As she catalogues them—"two lips, indifferent red . . . two grey eyes, with lids to them"—she ridicules the wooer's praises; but at the same time, it may not be too much to suggest, she robs her womanhood of its incipient animation.

Yet the cloistress has removed her veil and presently there is the ring. Orsino again sent no ring, but that need not prevent Olivia from returning it. And with this ruse the ring no less than the picture takes on a new significance. By means of it Olivia rejects Orsino's love but at the same time declares her own. And as Malvolio flings the ring upon the stage it makes its little dramatic *éclat.*[4] . . .

MALVOLIO—A CONTRAST TO OLIVIA

There is one character in the play who, unlike Olivia and Orsino, is unable to make this journey.[5] And that brings me to the subplot. . . . The love-delusions of Malvolio, brilliant as they are, fall into perspective as a parody of the more delicate aberrations of his mistress and her suitor. Like them Malvolio aspires towards an illusory ideal of love, but his mistake is a grosser one than theirs, his posturings more extravagant and grotesque. So *his* illusion enlarges the suggestions of the main plot about the mind's capacity for self-deception. . . .

The comparison between Olivia and Malvolio is one that the play specifically invites. He is the trusted steward of her household, and he suits her, she says, by being "sad and civil." This reminds us that it was with her authority that he descended on the midnight revels to quell that "uncivil rule." Have you no manners, he demands of Sir Toby and his crew; and his rebuke is one that Olivia herself will echo later when she calls Sir Toby a barbarian fit to dwell in "caves Where manners ne'er were preached." But if Olivia and Malvolio are united in seeking to impose an ordered regimen on these unruly elements, that does not mean, though I have found it

4. peal or sound   5. toward living and wisdom

said, that they share a doctrine of austerity.[6]. . . .

As the action proceeds, Olivia opens her heart to the new love that is being born within her, but Malvolio is only confirmed in that sickness of self-love of which she has accused him. . . . And Malvolio ends the play as he began by being called a fool. And if at first it was only the fool who called him so, now it is his mistress herself. Even as she pities him for the trick that has been played on him, "Alas, poor fool" are the words that Shakespeare puts into her mouth. . . .

What the comedy *may* suggest is that he who in his egotism seeks to fit the world to the procrustean bed[7] of his own reason deserves his own discomfiture. But Olivia, who self-confessedly abandons reason, and Orsino, who avidly gives his mind to all the shapes of fancy, are permitted to pass through whatever folly there may be in this to a greater illumination. Although what they sought has inevitably eluded them, it has nevertheless been vouchsafed to them in another form.

Yet it is the art of Shakespeare's comedy, and perhaps also its wisdom, to make no final judgments. The spirit of the piece, after all, is that of Twelfth Night and it is in the ideal world of Twelfth Night that Malvolio may be justly punished. Perhaps we should also remember, as even the Twelfth Night lovers do, to pause, if only for a moment, to recognize his precisian[8] virtues. Olivia agrees with him that he has been "notoriously abused" and the poet-lover Orsino sends after him to "entreat him to a peace," before they finally enter into the happiness to which "golden time" will summon them. "Golden time"—the epithet is characteristically Orsino's. It is only the wise fool who stays to sing to us about the rain that raineth every day.

6. strict and severe discipline   7. In Greek mythology, Procrustes had an iron bed. He put his victims on it and stretched them if they were too short and cut them off if they were too long.   8. strict and precise adherence to established rules, Puritan

Morality Lessons in *Twelfth Night*

John Hollander

John Hollander contends that *Twelfth Night* has a
moral: Excessive appetite for pleasure, when in-
dulged, eventually sickens and dies, and the natural
self emerges. His argument is based on two assumptions: first, that people can and do act in ways expected of them by forces outside of themselves and,
second, that people do have thoughts and feelings
which flow naturally from their minds and hearts,
but are subordinated by the roles they play. Hollander shows how the role-playing characters parallel
and contrast one another in pursuit of love, eating,
and music. Eventually, however, they tire of their
indulgence and give up their masques and disguises.
Finally, they emerge as fulfilled natural selves.
According to Hollander, all but two characters fit this
pattern. Feste, the clown, symbolizes revel and never
tires of any pleasure. Malvolio, on the other hand,
never seeks to indulge his appetite and tries to stand
above the others with a critical eye. At the end, he
fails to find fulfillment in his real self.
Based on Hollander's analysis, Shakespeare suggests in
Twelfth Night that indulgence, not abstinence, leads to reality, a point of view different from his contemporaries, who
satirize indulgence. John Hollander is an American poet,
critic, and editor. With Frank Kermode, he edited the *Oxford Anthology of English Literature.* He has published several short articles on Shakespeare's works.

The Action of *Twelfth Night* is indeed that of a Revels, a sus-
pension of mundane affairs during a brief epoch in a temporary world of indulgence, a land full of food, drink, love,
play, disguise and music. But parties end, and the reveller

John Hollander, "*Twelfth Night* and the Morality of Indulgence." First published in the
Sewanee Review, vol. 67, no. 2, Spring 1959. Copyright 1959, 1987 by the University of
the South. Reprinted with permission of the editor and author.

eventually becomes satiated and drops heavily into his worldly self again. The fact that plays were categorized as "revells" for institutional purposes may have appealed to Shakespeare; he seems at any rate to have analyzed the dramatic and moral nature of feasting, and to have made it the subject of his play. His analysis is schematized in Orsino's opening speech.

POPULARITY OF THE HUMORS

Shakespeare wrote Twelfth Night *when the concept of the humors was popular. In* Shakespeare: The Complete Works, *editor G.B. Harrison explains the history and meaning of humors.*

But the "humors" of the body were obviously of different kinds, and on the assumption that the physical body must be composed of four elements, "earth" was identified as black bile, "air" as blood, "fire" as bile, and "water" as phlegm. Each element produced a corresponding temperament, which was indicated outwardly by a man's complexion. Too much earth produced the *melancholic* humor; air, the *sanguine*; fire, the *choleric*; water, the *phlegmatic.*

In a healthy body the four humors were accurately balanced, one against the other; but if one humor became predominant or deficient, the individual became mentally and physically unbalanced.

In the 1590's the word "humor" rapidly became popular, as words sometimes will, and every intelligent person began to talk of his humors. Indeed, it became the mark of a would-be intellectual to have a humor, preferably melancholic, which was the sign of a great mind....

In Shakespeare's plays the word "humor" is very common and has a wide range of meanings. It may be used literally to mean moisture, or to imply one of the four humors, but its commonest meanings are whim, obsession, temperament, mood, temper, or inclination.

The essential action of a revels is: To so surfeit the Appetite upon excess that it "may sicken and so die." It is the Appetite, not the whole Self, however, which is surfeited: the Self will emerge at the conclusion of the action from where it has been hidden. The movement of the play is toward this emergence of humanity from behind a mask of comic type.

Act 1, scene 1, is very important as a statement of the nature of this movement. Orsino's opening line contains the play's three dominant images:

> If music be the food of love, play on.
> Give me excess of it, that, surfeiting,
> The appetite may sicken, and so die.   (act 1, scene 1)

Love, eating, and music are the components of the revelry, then. . . .

What is most important is that neither Feste, the feaster embodying not the spirit but the action of revelry, nor Malvolio, the ill-wisher (and the *bad appetite* as well), his polar opposite, appears in these introductory scenes. It is only upstairs in Olivia's house that the action as such commences. The revel opens with Feste's exchange with Maria in which she attempts three times to insist on innocent interpretations of "well-hanged" and "points." But Feste is resolute in his ribaldry. Thus Olivia, momentarily voicing Malvolio's invariable position, calls Feste a "dry fool," and "dishonest"; Malvolio himself refers to him as a "barren rascal." From here on in it will be Feste who dances attendance on the revelry, singing, matching wit with Viola, and being paid by almost everyone for his presence. To a certain degree he remains outside the action, not participating in it because he represents its very nature; occasionally serving as a comic angel or messenger, he is nevertheless unmotivated by any appetite, and is never sated of his fooling. His insights into the action are continuous, and his every remark is telling, "*Cucullus non facit monachum.*[1] That's as much as to say I wear not motley in my brain." Indeed, he does not, but more important is the fact that his robe and beard are not to make him a *real* priest later on. And neither he as Sir Thopas, nor Olivia as a "cloistress," nor Malvolio in his black suit of travestied virtue, nor the transvestite Viola is what he appears to be. No one will be revealed in his true dress until he has doffed his mask of feasting. And although neither Feste nor Malvolio will change in this respect, it is for completely opposite reasons that they will not do so. . . .

MALVOLIO OFFERS AN APPROACH TO THE PLAY'S MORAL NATURE

The moral nature of the plot of *Twelfth Night* can be easily approached through the character of Malvolio. . . . In the

---

1. "a cowl does not make a monk," *Measure for Measure,* act 5, scene 1

context of the play's moral physiology, his disease is shown forth as a case of indigestion due to his self-love, the result of a perverted, rather than an excessive appetite. In the world of feasting, the values of the commercial society outside the walls of the party go topsy-turvy: Feste is given money for making verbal fools of the donors thereof; everyone's desire is fulfilled in an unexpected way; and revellers are shown to rise through realms of unreality, disguise and luxurious self-deception. We are seduced, by the revelling, away from seeing the malice in the plot to undo Malvolio. But whatever malice there is remains peculiarly just. It is only Malvolio who bears any ill-will, and only he upon whom ill-will can appear to be directed. He makes for himself a hell of the worldly heaven of festivity, and when Toby and Maria put him into darkness, into a counterfeit-hell, they are merely representing in play a condition that he has already achieved.

The plot against Malvolio, then, is no more than an attempt to let him surfeit on himself, to present him with those self-centered, "time-pleasing" objects upon which his appetite is fixed. In essence, he is led to a feast in which his own vision of himself is spread before him, and commanded to eat it. . . .

But he continues to aspire to scholarship. In order to "let his tongue tang" with arguments of state, he intends to "read politic authors." His intrusion on the scene of Toby's and Andrew's merry-making involves a most significant remark: "Is there no respect of persons, time or place in you?" he asks. In other words, "Do you not observe even the dramatic unities in your revelling? Can you not apply even the values that govern things as frivolous as plays to your lives?" Coming from Malvolio, the ethical theorist, the remark feels very different from the remark made to Sir Toby by Maria, the practical moralist: "Aye, but you must confine yourself within the modest levels of order." Maria, presiding over the festivities, would keep things from getting out of hand. . . .

CHARACTERS CONTRAST AND PARALLEL ONE ANOTHER

For Malvolio there can be no fulfillment in "one self king." His story effectively and ironically underlines the progress toward this fulfillment in everybody else, and helps to delineate the limitations of the moral domain of the whole play. In contrast to Feste, who appears in the action at times as an abstracted spirit of revelry, Malvolio is a model of the sinner. The whole play abounds in such contrasts and parallels of character, and the players form and regroup continually with respect to these. . . .

Orsino also gives us a curious version of the physiology of the passions on which the plot is based; it is only relatively accurate, of course, for he will be the last of the revellers to feel stuffed, to push away from him his heaping dish.

> There is no woman's sides
> Can bide the beating of so strong a passion
> As love doth give my heart, no woman's heart
> So big to hold so much. They lack retention.
> Alas, their love may be called appetite—
> No motion of the liver,[2] but the palate—
> They suffer surfeit, cloyment and revolt.
> But mine is all as hungry as the sea
> And can digest as much.   (act 2, scene 4)

Viola has been giving him her "inside" throughout the scene, and were he not still ravenous for Olivia's love he could see her for what she is: a woman with a constancy in love (for himself and her brother) that he can only imagine himself to possess. She is indeed an Allegory of Patience on some baroque tomb at this point. She is ironically distinguished from Olivia in that her "smiling at grief" is a disguising "outside" for her real sorrow, whereas Olivia's is a real self-indulgent pleasure taken at a grief outworn. It is as if Olivia had misread Scripture and taken the letter of "Blessed are they that mourn" for the spirit of it. Her grief is purely ceremonial.

The "lighter people," too, are engaged in carrying out the action in their own way, and they have more business in the play than merely to make a gull of Malvolio. Toby's huge stomach for food and drink parallels the Duke's ravenous capacity for sentiment. The drinking scene is in one sense the heart of the play. . . .

FESTE: SONGSTER AND SYMBOL OF THE REVELS

When Toby and Andrew cry out for a love song, Feste obliges them, not with the raucous and bawdy thing that one would expect, but instead, with a direct appeal to their actual hostess, Olivia. This is all the more remarkable in that it is made on behalf of everyone in the play. "O Mistress Mine" under-

---

2. true passion

cuts the Duke's overwhelming but ineffectual mouthings, Viola's effective but necessarily misdirected charming, and, of course, Aguecheek's absolute incompetence as a suitor. . . .

Feste's other songs differ radically from "O Mistress Mine." He sings for the Duke a kind of languorous ayre, similar to so many that one finds in the songbooks. It is aimed at Orsino in the very extravagance of its complaint. It is his own song, really, if we imagine him suddenly dying of love, being just as ceremoniously elaborate in his funeral instructions as he has been in his suit of Olivia. And Feste's bit of handy-dandy to Malvolio in his prison is a rough-and-tumble sort of thing, intended to suggest in its measures a scrap from a Morality,[3] plainly invoking Malvolio in darkness as a devil in hell. Feste shows himself throughout the play to be a master of every convention of fooling.

If Feste's purpose is to serve as a symbol of the revels, however, he must also take a clear and necessary part in the all-important conclusion. *Twelfth Night* itself, the feast of the Epiphany,[4] celebrates the discovery of the "True King" in the manger by the Wise Men. "Those wits," says Feste in act 1, scene 5, "that think they have thee [wit] do very oft prove fools, and I that am sure I lack thee may pass for a wise man." And so it is that under his influence the true Caesario, the "one self king," is revealed. . . . But we have been dealing with the Action of *Twelfth Night* as representing the killing off of excessive appetite through indulgence of it, leading to the rebirth of the unencumbered self. The long final scene, then, serves to show forth the Caesario-King, and to unmask, discover and reveal the fulfilled selves in the major characters. . . .

THE SURFEITING HAS BEGUN

That the surfeiting has gradually begun to occur, however, has become evident earlier. In the prison scene, Sir Toby has already begun to tire: "I would we were well rid of this knavery." He gives as his excuse for this the fact that he is already in enough trouble with Olivia, but such as this has not deterred him in the past. And, in the last scene, very drunk as he must be, he replies to Orsino's inquiry as to his condition that he hates the surgeon, "a drunken rogue." Self-knowledge has touched Sir Toby. He could not have said this earlier.

As the scene plays itself out, Malvolio alone is left unac-

3. a kind of play popular in medieval times   4. a Christian feast celebrated on January 6

counted for. There is no accounting for him here, though; he remains a bad taste in the mouth. "Alas poor fool," says Olivia. "How have they baffled thee!" And thus, in Feste's words, "the whirligig of time brings in his revenges." Malvolio has become the fool, the "barren rascal." He leaves in a frenzy, to "be revenged," he shouts, "on the whole pack of you." He departs from the world of this play to resume a role in another, perhaps. His business has never been with the feasting to begin with, and now that it is over, and the revellers normalized he is revealed as the true madman. He is "The Madly-Used Malvolio" to the additional degree that his own uses have been madness.

For Orsino and Viola the end has also arrived. She will be "Orsino's mistress and his fancy's queen." He has been surfeited of his misdirected voracity; the rich golden shaft, in his own words, "hath killed the flock of all affections else" that live in him. "Liver, brain and heart" are indeed all supplied; for both Olivia and himself, there has been fulfillment in "one self king." And, lest there be no mistake, each is to be married to a Caesario or king. Again, "Liver, brain and heart" seems to encompass everybody: Toby and Maria are married, Aguecheek chastened, etc.

At the end of the scene, all exit. Only Feste, the pure fact of feasting, remains. His final song is a summation of the play in many ways at once. . . . The "swaggering" and incessant drunkenness of the following strophes[5] bring Man into prime and dotage, respectively. Lechery, trickery, dissembling and drunkenness, inevitable and desperate in mundane existence, however, are just those activities which, mingled together in a world of feasting, serve to purge Man of the desire for them. The wind and the rain accompany him throughout his life, keeping him indoors with "dreams and imaginations" as a boy, pounding and drenching him unmercifully, when he is locked out of doors, remaining eternal and inevitable throughout his pride in desiring to perpetuate himself. The wind and the rain are the most desperate of elements, that pound the walls and batter the roof of the warm house that shuts them out, while, inside it, the revels are in progress. Only after the party is ended can Man face them without desperation.

5. stanzas

THE METAPHOR OF THE RAIN

It is the metaphor of the rain that lasts longest, though, and it recapitulates the images of water, elements and humours[6] that have pervaded the entire play. Feste himself, who tires of nothing, addresses Viola: "Who you are and what you would are out of my welkin[7]—I might say 'element' but the word is overworn.". . . And finally, when all is done, "The rain it raineth every day," and Feste reverts to gnomic utterance[8] in a full and final seriousness. Water is rain that falls to us from Heaven. The world goes on. Our revels now are ended, but the actors solidify into humanity, in this case. "But that's all one, our play is done/And we'll strive to please you every day."

---

6. the four fluids of the body whose proportions were thought to determine a person's disposition   7. literally sky, upper air; here not of my kind   8. aphorisms, wise sayings

CHAPTER 4

Shakespeare's Final Plays

READINGS ON
THE COMEDIES

Shakespeare's Mastery Is Evident in the Last Plays

Edward Dowden

Edward Dowden argues that in all of the last plays, Shakespeare has achieved objectivity in his portrayal of both experienced adults and innocent children. Dowden notes that Prospero in *The Tempest* best exemplifies the characteristics his playwright-creator has achieved. These include inner harmony, mastery over intellect and emotions, sensitivity to wrong and commitment to justice, and a wise distance from the joys and sorrows of the world. Both character and creator know that freedom comes from service and art from discipline made light by imagination. During the late nineteenth century, Edward Dowden was professor of English literature at the University of Dublin, Ireland, and vice president of The New Shakespeare Society.

In the latest plays of Shakspere the sympathetic reader can discern unmistakably a certain abandonment of the common joy of the world, a certain remoteness from the usual pleasures and sadnesses of life, and, at the same time, all the more, this tender bending over those who are, like children, still absorbed in their individual joys and sorrows. Over the beauty of youth and the love of youth there is shed, in these plays of Shakspere's final period, a clear yet tender luminousness not elsewhere to be perceived in his writings. . . .

In these latest plays, the beautiful pathetic light is always present. There are the sufferers, aged, experienced, tried— Queen Katharine, Prospero, Hermione. And over against these there are the children, absorbed in their happy and exquisite egoism—Perdita and Miranda, Florizel and Ferdi-

From Edward Dowden, *Shakespeare: A Critical Study of His Mind and Art* (New York: Harper & Brothers, 1880).

nand, and the boys of old Belarius.[1]

The same means to secure ideality for these figures, so young and beautiful, is in each case (instinctively, perhaps, rather than deliberately) resorted to. They are lost children—princes, or a princess, removed from the court and its conventional surroundings into some scene of rare, natural beauty. There are the lost princes—Arviragus and Guiderius—among the mountains of Wales, drinking the free air and offering their salutations to the risen sun. There is Perdita, the shepherdess-princess, "queen of curds and cream," sharing, with old and young, her flowers, lovelier and more undying than those that Proserpina let fall from Dis's wagon.[2] There is Miranda (whose very name is significant of wonder), made up of beauty and love and womanly pity, neither courtly nor rustic, with the breeding of an island of enchantment, where Prospero is her tutor and protector, and Caliban her servant, and the Prince of Naples her lover. In each of these plays we can see Shakspere, as it were, tenderly bending over the joys and sorrows of youth. . . .

PROSPERO IDENTIFIED WITH SHAKESPEARE

It is not chiefly because Prospero is a great enchanter, now about to break his magic staff, to drown his book deeper than ever plummet sounded, to dismiss his airy spirits, and to return to the practical service of his Dukedom, that we identify Prospero in some measure with Shakspere himself. It is rather because the temper of Prospero, the grave harmony of his character, his self-mastery, his calm validity of will, his sensitiveness to wrong, his unfaltering justice, and, with these, a certain abandonment, a remoteness from the common joys and sorrows of the world, are characteristic of Shakspere as discovered to us in all his latest plays. Prospero is an harmonious and fully developed *will*. In the earlier play of fairy enchantments, *A Midsummer-Night's Dream*, the "human mortals" wander to and fro in a maze of error, misled by the mischievous frolic of Puck, the jester and clown of Fairy-land. But here the spirits of the elements, and Caliban, the gross genius of brute matter—needful for the service of life—are brought under subjection to the human will of Prospero. . . .

---

1. The characters come from several Shakespeare plays. 2. In Greek mythology, Proserpina was stolen by Hades (Pluto) to be his wife in the underworld. *Dis* means rich, another name for Hades.

And Prospero has reached not only the higher levels of moral attainment; he has also reached an altitude of thought from which he can survey the whole of human life, and see how small and yet how great it is. His heart is sensitive; he is profoundly touched by the joy of the children with whom, in the egoism of their love, he passes for a thing of secondary interest; he is deeply moved by the perfidy[3] of his brother. His brain is readily set a-work, and can with difficulty be checked from eager and excessive energizing; he is subject to the access of sudden and agitating thought. But Prospero masters his own sensitiveness, emotional and intellectual:

> We are such stuff
> As dreams are made on, and our little life
> Is rounded with a sleep. Sir, I am vex'd;
> Bear with my weakness; my old brain is troubled:
> Be not disturb'd with my infirmity;
> If you be pleased, retire into my cell
> And there repose; a turn or two I'll walk,
> To still my beating mind.   (act 4, scene 3)

"Such stuff as dreams are made on." Nevertheless, in this little life, in this dream, Prospero will maintain his dream rights and fulfil his dream duties. In the dream, he, a Duke, will accomplish Duke's work. Having idealized everything, Shakspere left everything real. . . .

TRUE FREEDOM COMES FROM SERVICE

A thought which seems to run through the whole of *The Tempest*, appearing here and there like a colored thread in some web, is the thought that the true freedom of man consists in service. Ariel, untouched by human feeling, is panting for his liberty. In the last words of Prospero are promised his enfranchisement and dismissal to the elements. Ariel reverences his great master, and serves him with bright alacrity; but he is bound by none of our human ties, strong and tender, and he will rejoice when Prospero is to him as though he never were. To Caliban, a land-fish, with the duller elements of earth and water in his composition, but no portion of the higher elements, air and fire, though he receives dim intimations of a higher world—a musical humming, or a twangling or a voice heard in sleep—to Caliban, service is slavery. He hates to bear his logs; he fears the incomprehensible power of Prospero, and obeys and curses. The great

3. violation of trust

master has usurped the rights of the brute-power Caliban. . . .

But while Ariel and Caliban, each in his own way, is impatient of service, the human actors, in whom we are chiefly interested, are entering into bonds—bonds of affection, bonds of duty, in which they find their truest freedom. Ferdinand and Miranda emulously contend in the task of bearing the burden which Prospero has imposed upon the prince:

> I am in my condition
> A prince, Miranda; I do think, a king:
> I would, not so! and would no more endure
> This wooden slavery than to suffer
> The flesh-fly blow my mouth. Hear my soul speak:
> The very instant that I saw you, did
> My heart fly to your service; there resides,
> To make me slave to it; and for your sake
> Am I this patient log-man.   (act 3, scene 2)

And Miranda speaks with the sacred candor from which spring the nobler manners of a world more real and glad than the world of convention and proprieties and pruderies:

> Hence, bashful cunning!
> And prompt me, plain and holy innocence!
> I am your wife, if you will marry me;
> If not, I'll die your maid: to be your fellow
> You may deny me; but I'll be your servant,
> Whether you will or no.
> FER.   My mistress, dearest;
> And I thus humble ever.
> MIR.   My husband, then?
> FER. Ay, with a heart as willing
> As bondage e'er of freedom."   (act 3, scene 2)

PROSPERO SYMBOLIZES SHAKESPEARE'S GENIUS, ART, AND DISCIPLINE

. . . If I were to allow my fancy to run out in play after such an attempted interpretation, I should describe Prospero as the man of genius, the great artist, lacking at first in practical gifts which lead to material success, and set adrift on the perilous sea of life, in which he finds his enchanted island, where he may achieve his works of wonder. He bears with him Art in its infancy—the marvellous child, Miranda. The grosser passions and appetites—Caliban—he subdues to his service:

> MIR.   'Tis a villain, sir,
> I do not love to look on.
> PROS.   But as 'tis,
> We cannot miss him.

MASTERY OVER WORDS

In his introduction to The Tempest *in* Shakespeare: The
Complete Works, *editor G.B. Harrison agrees with Dowden
that Shakespeare has achieved deep wisdom in the last plays
and asserts that* The Tempest *also epitomizes Shakespeare's
mastery over words.*

In *The Tempest*, Shakespeare has finally achieved complete mastery over words in the blank-verse form. This
power is shown throughout the play, but particularly in
some of Prospero's greatest speeches, such as "Our revels
now are ended," or in his farewell to his art. There is in
these speeches a kind of organ note not hitherto heard.
Shakespeare's thought was as deep as in his tragedies, but
now he was able to express each thought with perfect
meaning and its own proper harmony. Of his comedies,
certainly *The Tempest* is Shakespeare's greatest dramatic
poem. Unlike some of his other plays, it is better in the
reading than on the stage.

[Ferdinand's] winning of Miranda must not be too light and
easy. It shall be Ferdinand's task to remove some thousands
of logs and pile them according to the strict injunction of
Prospero. "Don't despise drudgery and dryasdust work,
young poets," Shakspere would seem to say, who had himself so carefully labored over his English and Roman histories; "for Miranda's sake such drudgery may well seem
light." Therefore, also, Prospero surrounds the marriage of
Ferdinand to his daughter with a religious awe. Ferdinand
must honor her as sacred, and win her by hard toil. But the
work of the higher imagination is not drudgery.... Prospero's departure from the island is the abandoning by
Shakspere of the theatre, the scene of his marvellous works:

> Graves, at my command,
> Have waked their sleepers, oped, and let them forth,
> By my so potent art.

Henceforth Prospero is but a man—no longer a great enchanter. He returns to the dukedom he had lost, in Stratford-
upon-Avon, and will pay no tribute henceforth to any Alonzo
or Lucy of them all.

Thus one may be permitted to play with the grave subject
of *The Tempest*; and I ask no more credit for the interpretation here proposed than is given to any other equally inno-

cent, if trifling, attempt to read the supposed allegory.

Shakspere's work, however, will, indeed, not allow itself to be lightly treated. The prolonged study of any great interpreter of human life is a discipline. Our loyalty to Shakspere must not lead us to assert that the discipline of Shakspere will be suitable to every nature. He will deal rudely with heart and will and intellect, and lay hold of them in unexpected ways, and fashion his disciple, it may be, in a manner which at first is painful and almost terrible. . . .

"'The true question to ask,' says the Librarian of Congress, in a paper read before the Social Science Convention at New York, October, 1869—'The true question to ask respecting a book is, *Has it helped any human soul?*' This is the hint, statement, not only of the great Literatus,[4] his book, but of every great artist.". . .

SHAKESPEARE OFFERS COURAGE, ENERGY, AND STRENGTH

There is an admirable sentence by Emerson: "A good reader can in a sort nestle into Plato's brain, and think from thence; but not into Shakspere's. We are still out of doors."

We are still out of doors; and, for the present, let us cheerfully remain in the large, good space. Let us not attenuate Shakspere to a theory. He is careful that we shall not thus lose our true reward: "The secrets of nature have not more gift in taciturnity."[5] Shakspere does not supply us with a doctrine, with an interpretation, with a revelation. What he brings to us is this—to each one, courage and energy and strength to dedicate himself and his work to that, whatever it be, which life has revealed to him as best and highest and most real.

---

4. Latin for one learned in literature   5. *Troilus and Cressida*, act 4, scene 2

Similarities Between *Measure for Measure* and *The Tempest*

Harold S. Wilson

Harold S. Wilson argues that many parallels exist between Shakespeare's plays *Measure for Measure* and *The Tempest*, treating the former as a source for the latter play. Dukes set in motion the action of both plays, but because neither duke controls anyone else's choices, both can only try to influence others to make moral choices. According to Wilson, the choices relate to the theme of the two plays—the virtues of repentance, forgiveness, and justice with mercy. Consequently, both dukes are agents of moral order and represent authority. As the dukes are temporal, or earthly, rulers with a duty to follow the Scriptures, Wilson says, the plays subtly remind reader and audience that life is transitory. Though *The Tempest* is richer in spectacle and poetic imagery, Wilson thinks the action of *Measure for Measure* is more moving. Harold S. Wilson is a member of the English department at the University of Toronto and serves on the editorial board of the *Shakespeare Quarterly*. He has published critical articles on Shakespeare's works in journals and periodicals.

If we compare the dramatic methods of *Measure for Measure* and *The Tempest* with reference to the directing roles that their two dukes play—Vincentio of Vienna and Prospero of Milan and the Magic Island—we may observe a notable difference in their procedures. Both of them seem to supervise and control the action of their respective plays. But whereas Prospero takes us immediately into his confidence and explains his purpose as he goes along, Duke Vincentio never ex-

Harold S. Wilson, "Action and Symbol in *Measure for Measure* and the *Tempest*," *Shakespeare Quarterly*, vol. 4 (1953). Reprinted by permission of the *Shakespeare Quarterly*.

plicitly states his purpose in *Measure for Measure* and we are left to deduce it from the course and outcome of the action. . . .

THE ROLES OF THE TWO DUKES

In *The Tempest,* Shakespeare uses essentially the same design[1] but he alters his narrative method. Prospero explains his purposes, during the course of the action, as overtly as the Duke of *Measure for Measure* conceals his. The dramatic situation, too, is handled differently. *Measure for Measure* shows an action *ab ovo,* from its inception through the appointment of Angelo as the Duke's deputy to the general pardon at the end; whereas *The Tempest* shows only the end of an action, the turning point of which has been achieved before the play opens. The wrong suffered by Prospero occurred when Miranda was a child of three. During the years while Miranda has been growing up, Prospero has been maturing his magic arts and biding the moment appointed that shall deliver his enemies into his hands. He has had ample time to digest his resentment and examine his conscience; and his magic has become so powerful that it must serve as an instrument of great evil or great good.

The real conflict of the play's design is the moral conflict of Prospero, but the play itself shows us only the benevolent results of its resolution. The terms of its resolution are marked for us just before the climax, in Prospero's words to Ariel:

Though with their high wrongs I am struck to th' quick,
Yet with my nobler reason 'gainst my fury
Do I take part. The rarer action is
In virtue than in vengeance.[2] They being penitent,
The sole drift[3] of my purpose doth extend
Not a frown further. . . .   (act 5, scene 1)

But his choice has been made before the play opens, as the earlier acts imply. The spectacular storm scene with which the play begins is immediately explained as part of Prospero's design:

Tell your piteous heart
There's no harm done,

he says to Miranda. We listen, with her, to the account of its causes, and learn from the following dialogue with Ariel (act 1, scene 2) what to expect in the ensuing scenes.

This is the epitome of the method used throughout. We

1. as in *Measure for Measure*   2. It is a finer action to be self-controlled than to take vengeance.   3. intention

witness a succession of spectacles and pseudo-conflicts, preceded or accompanied by the explanatory comment of Prospero. In place of the real conflict of Prospero's choice, we have the balanced pseudo-conflicts of Antonio's design to make Sebastian King of Naples, and the drunken efforts of Caliban and the clowns to become lords of the isle. But we are in no suspense about the outcome of either, for we see (and Prospero himself repeatedly informs us [in acts 3 and 4]) that there is no resisting his magic; it paralyzes his opponents, deprives them of reason and boils their brains within their skulls; Caliban and his companions are wracked with cramps and dance up to their chins in the filthy-mantled pool beyond Prospero's cell. In the awakening love of Ferdinand and Miranda, Prospero similarly instructs us concerning his purpose and tactics, though here his magic consists simply in the psychology of opposition and the choice remains the lovers' own.

When we reflect upon it, we cannot help noticing how close the parallel is with *Measure for Measure*. In each play, the action is set going and guided throughout by its duke; yet neither Duke Vincentio nor Prospero controls anyone else's choice; rather, they prepare the conditions in which others choose while taking precautions that no one shall give effect to a choice injurious to others. As Vincentio guides Claudio and Angelo to choose penitence and Isabella to prefer mercy to revenge or justice, so Prospero guides Alonso to choose penitence, Ferdinand to choose the love of Miranda, while he himself forgoes revenge or even justice in favor of mercy; and even Caliban shows signs of amendment at the end. As Barnardine and Lucio in *Measure for Measure* are given the chance to repent, though they remain unmoved, so with Antonio and Sebastian; but though all four are pardoned, they are also curbed of their evil propensities.

The parallelism is not precise—nor should we expect it to be; Shakespeare does not repeat himself—but it is fundamental, arising as it does out of the identical ruling conception of the two plays: the virtue of forgiveness and the tempering of justice with mercy; and the parallel may be carried further. In the two dukes, there is the suggestion of an earlier unworldliness and a consequent failure to anticipate evil or cope with it—Prospero in failing to anticipate his brother's plot against him, Vincentio in failing to curb the evil conditions of Vienna. When each duke begins to act effectively, his conduct seems to invoke a certain supernatural aid and sanction. Duke Vincentio's arrangements are compared with the operation of Divine Grace (*Measure for Measure*, act 5, scene 1), while Prospero's "white magic" is explained as divinely sanctioned: Ariel and his fellows are "ministers of fate" (act 3, scene 3), and their powers cannot be used to serve an evil purpose, as Sycorax discovered.

Thus each duke is seen as the human agent who gives effect to the moral order of things as divinely authorized. And appropriately, after the wrongs have been righted and the reconciliations effected, Duke Vincentio lays aside his friar's robe and returns to his appointed role as ruler of Vienna; Prospero breaks his staff, drowns his book, and resumes his natural function as Duke of Milan. Prospero's method throughout *The Tempest* has been to deceive men for their own good; so with Duke Vincentio; and *The Tempest* shows us the same design of "measure for measure": the suffering visited upon Prospero is in turn meted to his enemies; but the grace that preserved Prospero also preserves them.

When each duke puts off his disguise and stands revealed in his true temporal status, the Duke of Vienna and the Duke of Milan, each is seen as a *temporal* authority, the good governor who knows how to mingle mercy with justice. Wilson Knight has associated *Measure for Measure* with the text: "Judge not, that ye be not judged," and has further written: "The central idea of *Measure for Measure* is this: 'And forgive us our debts as we forgive our debtors.' Thus 'justice' is a mockery: man, himself a sinner, cannot presume to judge. That is the lesson driven home in *Measure for Measure*." But this way of putting it overlooks an important point. Duke Vincentio and Duke Prospero are both temporal rulers; that is, to a sixteenth-century way of thought, they are divinely constituted authorities whose duty it is to rule and judge other men, according to the precept and example of Scripture, with justice and mercy. This is precisely the problem with which *Measure for Measure* deals, how to do this; and it is likewise the difficulty that confronts Prospero. Each of them solves the problem, though by different means. Duke Vincentio relies upon a conveniently impenetrable disguise and a certain ubiquitousness[4] that makes it possible for him to influence people's purposes strongly for good; and Prospero has his magic; but each of them stands revealed at the

4. existence everywhere at the same time

end in his proper role as an earthly ruler who judges his subjects with authority. Each is a type and model of the Christian governor.

Finally, each play contains a subtle implication of the transitoriness, the illusion, even, of the life it depicts. In *Measure for Measure*, this is faintly yet definitely implied through the sustained theatricality of the Duke's role and in his homily to the penitent Claudio, *de contemptu mundi*,[5] in act 3. In *The Tempest*, the theme becomes beautifully explicit in Prospero's famous lines at the end of the Masque of Ceres (act 4, scene 1), and in the epilogue. Here, the breaking of the dramatic illusion is deliberate. Before our very eyes, the great Duke of Milan and the mighty magician vanishes; Prospero stands before us as a poor player, who entreats our applause. The play itself has been "such stuff as dreams are made on."

These affiliations between the two plays can hardly be inadvertent on Shakespeare's part. *Measure for Measure* is an important "source" for *The Tempest*. The later play is a reworking of the theme of the former, employing a different dramatic method and calculated for a different dramatic effect. *Measure for Measure* is all action; *The Tempest* is largely spectacle invested with some of the finest poetry Shakespeare ever wrote. The significance of the one emerges from the pattern of the action, without commentary; of the other, from a succession of magic spells accompanied by the magician's interpretive comment. The method of *The Tempest* is less dramatic, less deeply moving, perhaps; it is pictorially static, "spatial," as Wilson Knight calls it; and this effect is in remarkable contrast with the temporal, dynamic movement of *Measure for Measure*. But the method of *The Tempest* affords very much greater scope for the decorating of the theme, with the panoply of the court masque, its gorgeous properties of costume and music and setting, graceful dances and tableaux, and the richer texture of poetic image and symbol. None of these compete with the action or the developing thought of *The Tempest*, made crystal clear in Prospero's explanations. In *Measure for Measure*, the method is indirect and more economical of decoration; and by the same token it is the more deeply stirring; the action contains the thought, the symbolic effect, which is achieved wholly by implication.

5. concerning contempt for the world

Three Themes in
The Tempest

Northrop Frye

Before elaborating on three themes in *The Tempest*, Northrop Frye clarifies major events in the play. In the past, Antonio usurped Prospero as duke of Milan and exiled him from the city to an island where Prospero dwells during the play. A great storm causes a shipwreck that brings Antonio and his party to the island. The play involves the quests, ordeals, and visions of the four groups of shipwrecked passengers and the Island dwellers. The theme of time, Frye says, haunts the play. Events disturb time's flow, extending or compressing it. At the end, a proper time releases them from the island. A second theme is nature; the play exists within an ordered nature in which transformations occur. A third theme explores illusion; according to Frye, Prospero's reality is illusion, a world of dreaming and magic. This illusion is Prospero's art, and art is the agent that transforms the characters. When the magic is over, Prospero asks to be released.

Northrop Frye received his education at the University of Toronto and Oxford University, earning degrees in philosophy, English, and theology. He began teaching English at Victoria College, University of Toronto, in 1939. He is the author of *The Educated Imagination*, *The Anatomy of Criticism*, and a study of William Blake's poetry.

The Tempest is certainly one of the late romances: it's also an unusually short play, one of the shortest in the canon.... This play presents only the second half of the full story. The first half is the story recounted by Prospero to Miranda in the second scene: a sombre tale of treachery in which he, as Duke of Milan, was deposed and exiled with her. If this is

Reprinted with permission from *Northrop Frye on Shakespeare*, edited by Robert Sandler (New Haven, CT: Yale University Press; Markham, ON: Fitzhenry Whiteside, 1986). Copyright 1986 by Northrop Frye.

right, it's not surprising that there seems to be no really convincing general source. . . .

Prospero was Duke of Milan, and appears to have been more or less useless at that job because he spent all his time reading books; nevertheless his people dearly loved him. We're well outside the realistic area already. His brother Antonio, at first through necessity, then through ambition, took over as regent, and finally, after making a deal with Alonso, King of Naples, an enemy of Prospero, felt strong enough to assume the title of Duke of Milan, sending Prospero and his three-year-old daughter, Miranda, in a leaky boat out to sea. . . .

Gonzalo, a Milanese courtier charged with outfitting the boat, supplied Prospero and Miranda with food, water, clothes and, above all, some books. As he can hardly have provided the books merely to give Prospero something to read while he drowns, he seems to have acted on an intuition that the boat might not sink after all. Although he was working for Antonio, he gets a great deal of credit for his charitable actions in the play, and if he did have such an intuition, he was right: the boat drifted to the shore of an island somewhere in the Mediterranean between Naples and Tunis.[1] Some of the books were evidently books of magic, grimoires and the like, and textbooks on astrology and alchemy.

THE STORM AND SHIPWRECK

A ship bearing Antonio and his confederate Alonso, along with Alonso's brother Sebastian and son Ferdinand, with Gonzalo and some other courtiers (an unnamed son of Antonio is also referred to, perhaps by a slip), is returning from Tunis from the wedding of Alonso's daughter Claribel. The first scene, in prose, describes the wrecking of the ship (more accurately the denuding it of passengers) by Prospero's magic. It's a brilliant scene of sailors cursing the passengers for getting in their way, Antonio and Sebastian cursing the sailors for trying to save their lives, and Gonzalo clinging to a hope that the Boatswain will be hanged and therefore not everybody will be drowned. . . .

Next comes a long, technically rather clumsy scene in which Prospero fills in Miranda about the story I just summarized, then calls in Ariel and Caliban and uses them to

1. on the northern coast of Africa

outline the earlier history of the island. We are told that when Prospero first came to the island it had been controlled by an evil witch named Sycorax, who had been banished there from Algiers because she was pregnant with what proved to be Caliban, and the pregnancy commuted her death sentence. The magic changes from black to white with Prospero. When we first read through the play, our attention is caught by a lovely speech by Caliban, not a person we'd associate with beautiful speeches as a rule, beginning "Be not afear'd; the isle is full of noises." What this speech appears to be telling us is that not all the magic on the island is directly controlled by Prospero, whose own magic seems to be used only to torment Caliban, so far as it's applied to him. The island, evidently, is a place of magic, harnessed or directed by Sycorax to bad ends and by Prospero to good ones.

The wrecked passengers are separated, mainly by Ariel's activity, into four main groups. Each, with one exception, goes through a quest, an ordeal and a symbolic vision. Ferdinand, the hero, goes in quest of his father, even though he's been told, through one of Ariel's songs, that his father is drowned. On the way he meets Miranda: Prospero oversees them, and pretends to be hostile to Ferdinand. The excuse he gives in an aside for this seems a very thin one, but in romances fathers of heroines regularly do go through phases of hostility to prospective sons-in-law. . . .

QUESTS, ORDEALS, AND VISIONS

So Ferdinand is given Caliban's job of carrying logs of wood. Apart from showing the necessity of including all the normal conventions of romance, this scene has another function. Everyone in the play is getting some sort of education as a result of the dramatic action, and the sight of Ferdinand, the third man in her experience, is important for Miranda's. When she and Prospero first visit Caliban, she makes a speech, beginning "Abhorrèd slave," in which she is simply parroting her father. (If your edition of *The Tempest* gives this speech to Prospero, throw it away.) But as soon as Ferdinand comes in sight, she takes his side against her father, and by the end of the scene she's apologizing to Ferdinand for her father's behaviour. . . .

The Court Party searches for Ferdinand, as Ferdinand does for them, convinced that he's drowned. This conviction, that everyone they don't see is dead, affects all the wrecked passengers in some way, and gives an eerie afterworld quality to the island. I've spoken of the island as having a magical quality of its own, apart from Prospero. . . .

PROSPERO'S FINAL PLEA

In the epilogue of The Tempest, *Prospero tells the audience that he has no more magic and asks the audience to release him with fervent applause.*

Now my charms are all o'erthrown,
And what strength I have's mine own,
Which is most faint. Now, 'tis true,
I must be here confined by you,
Or sent to Naples. Let me not,
Since I have my dukedom got,
And pardoned the deceiver, dwell
In this bare island by your spell,
But release me from my bands[1]
With the help of your good hands.[2]
Gentle breath[3] of yours my sails
Must fill, or else my project fails,
Which was to please. Now I want[4]
Spirits to enforce, art to enchant,
And my ending is despair
Unless I be relieved by prayer
Which pierces so that it assaults
Mercy itself, and frees all faults.
As you from crimes would pardoned be,
Let your indulgence set me free.

1. bonds   2. by clapping   3. kindly criticism   4. lack

In any case the ordeal of the Court Party is their exhausting wandering and the confinement that follows it, and their symbolic vision the banquet spread before them, which Ariel, descending in the form of a harpy,[2] snatches away from them, the vision being symbolic of deceitful desire. This vision, however, does not seem to be shared by Gonzalo, who apparently does not hear Ariel's speech: his vision is rather his private reverie in which he sees the island in the form of an ideal commonwealth, much to the amusement of Antonio and Sebastian.

---

2. in Greek mythology a voracious monster with the head and trunk of a woman and the tail, wings, and talons of a bird

Stephano and Trinculo fall in with Caliban and go on a quest to find Prospero, with the object of murdering him. Their ordeal is to fall into a horsepond and then to be hunted by spirit dogs; their symbolic vision is the "trumpery," evidently some fine-looking clothes, that Prospero hangs out for them to steal. We remember the word from *The Winter's Tale.* Caliban is not taken in by the "trumpery": perhaps his symbolic vision is the dream of music I mentioned earlier. Then there's the Boatswain and his crew, who don't get a chance to go on a quest of any kind, but are confined in what sounds like a noisy pit of hell, and then released to see their ship once more as good as new. Thus:

Character	Quest	Ordeal	Vision
Ferdinand	search for father	log bearing	masque
(a) Gonzalo	(a and b) search for	(a and b) "forthrights	(a) common-wealth
(b) "three men of sin"	Alonso's son	and meanders"	(b) harpy banquet
(a) Caliban	(a and b) search for	(a and b) horsepond	(a) dream of music
(b) Stephano Trinculo	Prospero		(b) "trumpery"
Boatswain and crew		imprisonment and noise	renewed ship

THE ELEMENT OF TIME

The Tempest is more haunted by the passing of time than any other play I know: I suspect that even its name is the Latin *tempestas*, meaning time as well as tempest, like its French descendant *temps*, which means both time and weather. This is partly because Prospero, as a magician, has to be a close watcher of time: his knowledge of the stars tells him when it's time to tell Miranda about her past ("The very minute bids thee ope thine ear"), and he also says to Miranda that his lucky star is in the ascendant, and unless he acts now he's lost his chance forever. All through the play he keeps reminding Ariel of the time, and Ariel himself, of course, is longing for his freedom, even "before the time be out." The right moment can also be associated with tragic or evil actions. . . . The proverb that time and tide wait for no man is constantly in the background: even though this is a Mediterranean island, there is much talk about tides and their movements. Tragic or evil time presents a moment for, so to speak, cutting into the flow of time. Antonio and Sebastian have no idea how they are to get off the island after they've murdered Alonso, but that doesn't matter: they must seize the moment. Comic time is more leisurely. . . .

Comic time can be leisurely, but it can also be very concentrated: Ferdinand and Miranda are united for life even though, as Alonso says, they can't have known each other more than three hours. Prospero does a good deal of fussing about keeping Miranda's virginity intact until after the ceremony: again the reason is more magical than moral. Unless things are done in the proper time and rhythm, everything will go wrong. The play is full of stopped action, like the charming of Ferdinand's and Antonio's swords; and the Court Party, Ariel says to Prospero, "cannot budge till your release." The theme of release spreads over all the characters in the final recognition scene, including the release of Ariel into the elements, and carries on into Prospero's Epilogue, when he asks the audience to release him by applause. . . .

A TRANSFORMATION WITHIN NATURE

But magic in its turn is a binding of nature, and the speech in which Prospero renounces his magic represents the release of nature as well. Sycorax was an evil magician, and the traditional attribute of the witch, since Virgil at least, was the drawing down of the moon. . . . But *The Tempest*, except for Ariel, does not move out of the normal natural order: even Caliban, though the son of a witch, is human. The action of the play is a transformation within nature. . . .

At the bottom of the ladder of nature, as far as this play is concerned, is Caliban. No character in Shakespeare retains more dignity under so constant a stream of abuse. Nobody seems even to know what shape he is: he is constantly called a fish, but that seems a judgment by nose rather than eyesight. I was once asked by a former student, now a teacher, how I would costume Caliban, and was startled to realize that I hadn't a clue. Most of the productions I've seen make him look like a very imperfectly trained seal. He is clearly deformed, whether a "monster" or not, and he is clearly a savage. The worst handicap for a savage, Shakespeare's contemporaries would feel, is idolatry. Caliban has been supplied with a god named Setebos by his mother, and when Stephano appears with his wine bottle he makes a god out of him, a sort of Dionysus dropped from the moon. But he outgrows that too, and his last speech in the play indicates a genuinely human ambition to "seek for grace." Prospero treats him in a way calculated to instil as much hatred for him in Caliban as possible: the excuse for doing so is that Prospero was originally kind to Caliban, until he tried to rape Miranda. There seem to be things about nature that even Prospero doesn't know. What Prospero means, other than the fact that Caliban belongs on the island, when he says "this thing of darkness I/Acknowledge mine," we're not sure, nor do we know if Prospero is likely to take Caliban along when he leaves the island. . . .

At the top of what we see of nature is the wedding masque, a lovely celebration of the fertility of nature and its relation to marriage presented by three goddesses of the earth, the sky and the rainbow. Venus, who is most active on a lower level of nature, is excluded from the action. The presence of the rainbow and the emphasis on the continued regularity of the seasons suggest a new world washed clean by the flood (a highly symbolic flood, naturally), and the references to a perpetual spring and autumn give us the attributes of an earthly paradise—in fact "paradise" is the word Ferdinand uses. The dance at the end is between nymphs of the brooks, who seem to represent spring, and harvesters of the autumn. . . .

REALITY AND ILLUSION

I've said that in a stage play reality and illusion are the same thing, and the action of *The Tempest* seems to show us both an illusion of reality and the reality of illusion. At the bottom level is the *Realpolitik*[3] of Antonio and Sebastian and their plot to murder Alonso, a plot parodied by Stephano's plot to murder Prospero. This is the way you're supposed to act in the "real world" to get along, but on this island such reality seems to be merely an illusion of greed. The quality of dreaming on the island also seems to be an index of character: we have Gonzalo's reverie on his ideal commonwealth

3. action or politics based on practical and material factors

and the dream in the speech of Caliban I mentioned. Every-thing that we think of as "real," everything physical, tangible and substantial around us, is, Prospero tells us in his great "Our revels now are ended" speech, an illusion that lasts a lit-tle longer than some other illusions. On the other hand, illu-sions, such as the songs of Ariel and the mirages seen by the Court Party, including the disappearing banquet, belong to Prospero's "art" and have a creative role, agents in the trans-formation of character. Most of Prospero's "art" in the play is magic, but some of it is also music and drama, and this "art" acts as a counter-illusion, the material world of an intelligi-ble or spiritual reality. We don't know how far Prospero in-tended actual revenge on his enemies at the beginning of the play: the care he took not to harm anyone suggests that he didn't. Still, it sounds a little as though Prospero were getting educated too, and specifically on the point that revenge is il-lusory counter-action, just as "the rarer action" which re-nounces revenge is the genuinely creative counter-illusion.

The books Gonzalo put into Prospero's boat are part of a collection that Prospero prizes above his dukedom, and per-haps the reason why Caliban's conspiracy infuriates him in-stead of amusing him is Caliban's hatred of his books, as the only sources of power he has. . . .

Prospero tells us that when he returns to Milan as Duke, "Every third thought shall be my grave." Doesn't sound like much of a prospect for Milan. W.H. Auden, in a dramatic poem based on *The Tempest* called *The Sea and the Mirror*, has Prospero remark to Ariel that he is particularly glad to have got back his dukedom at a time when he no longer wanted it. In the Epilogue Prospero tells us that he has used up all his magic, and the rest is up to us. We then hear him pleading for release, in a tone echoing the Lord's Prayer and going far beyond any conventional appeal for applause. How are we to release him?

In many tales of the *Tempest* type, the island sinks back into the sea when the magician leaves. But we, going out of the theatre, perhaps have it in our pockets like an apple: per-haps our children can sow the seeds in the sea and bring forth again the island that the world has been searching for since the dawn of history, the island that is both nature and human society restored to their original form, where there is no sovereignty and yet where all of us are kings.

GLOSSARY

alliteration: The repetition of consonant sounds, such as *b*lack *b*oughs.

ambiguity: A quality of meaning that allows lines to be interpreted in two or more ways, allowing the speaker to say more than one thing at a time.

blank verse: Unrhymed lines written in iambic pentameter, especially suitable to dramatic verse

burlesque: A form of comedy that derives its humor from a discrepancy between subject matter and style; the sublime made absurd, honest emotions turned into sentimentality, or frivolous subjects treated seriously.

caricature: The focus on a certain individual quality in a person, exaggerating and distorting it to create a ridiculous effect.

chorus: A part taken by a single actor who recites the prologue and epilogue and gives interact comments that link the acts and foreshadow coming events.

classical comedy: Usually the plays of ancient Greece and Rome, which are characterized by established tradition and recognized excellence; any comedy with a lasting tradition.

conceit: An elaborate and complex comparison.

denouement: The final unraveling of the plot in drama; the solution of the mystery and the explanation of the outcome.

epistemology, epistemological: Concerned with the study of the nature of knowledge.

epithet: An adjective or adjective phrase used to point out a characteristic of a person or thing, such as "love-struck Orlando."

exemplum, exempla (pl.): A tale that teaches a moral by illustration or example.

exposition: Introductory material in the structure of drama; it creates tone, gives setting, introduces characters, and supplies facts needed to understand the play.

farce: A dramatic piece intended to incite laughter by presenting exaggerated situations that depend on gross incongruities, coarse wit, or horseplay.

foil: A character that by contrast enhances or underscores the characteristics of another character.

frame setting: A narrative setting within which a story is told; also called an induction.

haute comedie: High or elegant comedy.

image or **imagery:** A word group that forms a picture or sound in the reader's or listener's mind.

irony: The use of words to state one message, while the phrasing indicates that the opposite meaning is intended.

low comedy: Comedy lacking in subtlety or serious purpose, characterized by quarreling, boasting, trickery, coarse jesting, noisy singing, and shrewishness.

masque: Dramatic entertainment as a scene within a play: characterized by elaborate costumes, singing, and dancing.

maxim: A short, concise saying usually stating practical advice; an adage.

melancholy: Sad or depressed spirits; gloomy.

melodrama: A play designed to keep the audience thrilled with scenes evoking strong feelings of pity, horror, or joy.

meter: The measured pattern of sound created by the repetition of accented and unaccented syllables.

motif: A recurring element that serves as a foundation in a drama.

paradox: A statement that seems contradictory or absurd, but that may actually be well founded or true.

parody: A work that imitates and exaggerates a serious work, usually to poke fun at an author and his or her style.

pastoral: Any art form that treats of shepherds and rustic country life, usually in an idyllic way.

persona: A voice or character representing the speaker or author.

personification: A poetic device attributing human qualities to nonhuman things.

prologue: A speech by a major character or a chorus before a play begins to provide the audience with the facts necessary for understanding the play.

repartee: A quick, witty response.

rhetorical devices: The various devices that make style effective or persuasive.

romantic comedy: A comedy characterized by serious love as the chief motive, much out-of-doors action, an idealized heroine, and love subjected to great difficulties.

sentimentalism: Overindulgence in emotion; failure to restrain or evaluate emotion through exercise of judgment; an optimistic overemphasis of the goodness of humanity.

simile: A figure of speech in which the similarity between two objects is stated with the word *like* or *as*.

soliloquy: A speech delivered while a character is alone onstage and calculated to inform the audience of the speaker's thoughts.

stock characters: Conventional, stereotypical characters, such as the melancholy man, the servant-confidant, the court fool, or the nagging wife.

symbolism: The use of symbols—images that suggest an idea or concept or emotion—in a work of art.

tableau, tableaux (pl.): A striking scene; an interlude during a scene when all performers on stage freeze in position and then resume action.

tone, tonalities: The implied attitude of a writer toward the subject and material of a play and the devices used to convey it.

trope: A figure of speech that marks a turn or change in the sense, such as using a word in a way other than its proper or literal sense.

vernacular: The common, everyday speech of the people; nonliterary language.

Chronology

1557

Shakespeare's parents, John Shakespeare and Mary Arden, marry

1558

Elizabeth I becomes queen of England

1561

Philosopher and statesman Francis Bacon born; advanced as actual writer of Shakespeare's plays by skeptics in modern age

1562

First English participation in New World slave trade from Africa

1564

William Shakespeare born

English dramatist Christopher Marlowe born

Italian painter, sculptor, and architect Michaelangelo dies at age eighty-eight

1569

John Shakespearc becomes bailiff of Stratford

CA. 1570

Emilia Bassano, daughter of a court musician and suggested real-life dark lady of the Sonnets, born

1572

Ben Jonson, English playwright and poet, born

1576

The Theatre, England's first playhouse, is built in London

1577–1580

Sir Francis Drake's first English voyage around the world

1578

Historian and printer Rafael Holinshed publishes *Chronicles of English History to 1575*, source of material for Shakespeare's histories

1582

Shakespeare marries Anne Hathaway

1583

Daughter Susanna born

1584

Sir Walter Raleigh founds Virginia colony on Roanoke Island

1585

Twins Hamnet and Judith born

1587

Execution of Mary, Queen of Scots, by order of Elizabeth I
Marlowe's *Tamburlaine* performed in London

1587–1590

Shakespeare acting and touring

1588

Spanish Armada defeated by British navy, making way for England's ascendancy in world trade and colonization

1591

1 Henry VI

1591–1592

2 and *3 Henry VI*

1592

Robert Greene attacks Shakespeare in print, the first known reference to Shakespeare's reputation or work
Galileo proves objects fall at the same rate regardless of their weight, in Pisa

1592–1593

The Comedy of Errors
Sonnets
Richard III

1593

Plague in London
Marlowe dies in tavern brawl
Titus Andronicus
The Taming of the Shrew
The Two Gentlemen of Verona

Love's Labour's Lost
Venus and Adonis published

1594

Lord Chamberlain's Men, Shakespeare's acting company, formed
The Rape of Lucrece published

1594–1595

A Midsummer Night's Dream
Romeo and Juliet
Richard II

1595–1596

The Merchant of Venice

1596

Shakespeare applies for and receives coat of arms in his father's name, achieves gentleman status
Hamnet Shakespeare dies
King John

1597

Shakespeare buys New Place, property in Stratford that becomes his family's home
1 Henry IV

1598

The Theatre torn down; timbers used for new Globe
2 Henry IV
Much Ado About Nothing

1599

Globe theater opens
Henry V
As You Like It
Julius Caesar
The Merry Wives of Windsor
"The Passionate Pilgrim" published

1600–1601

Twelfth Night
Hamlet
Troilus and Cressida

1601

John Shakespeare dies
"The Phoenix and the Turtle"

1602

Shakespeare buys land at Stratford
Othello

1603

Bubonic plague strikes London
Elizabeth I dies
James I becomes king of England
English conquest of Ireland
Lord Chamberlain's Men becomes King's Men
All's Well That Ends Well

1604

Measure for Measure

1605

Repression of Catholics and Puritans
Gunpowder Plot to kill James I and members of Parliament
Shakespeare invests in Stratford tithes
World's first newspaper begins publication in Antwerp

1606

Visit by king of Denmark
Ben Jonson's *Volpone*
King Lear
Macbeth

1607

Jamestown, Virginia, founded
Daughter Susanna marries Dr. John Hall

1607–1609

Antony and Cleopatra
Coriolanus
Timon of Athens (unfinished)
Pericles completed

1608

Plague in London
King's Men acquire Blackfriars theater
Granddaughter Elizabeth Hall born
Mary Arden Shakespeare dies

1609

Sonnets and "A Lover's Complaint" published by Thomas
    Thorpe, an edition believed unauthorized
Johannes Kepler proves planetary orbits are elliptical

1610

Cymbeline

1610–1611

The Winter's Tale

1611

The Maydenhead of the first musicke that ever was printed for the Virginalls, first book of keyboard music published in England
The King James Bible published
Shakespeare contributes to highway bill, repairing roads between Stratford and London
The Tempest

1612

Shakespeare's brother Gilbert dies

1612–1613

Henry VIII

1613

The Globe theater burns down
Shakespeare's brother Richard dies
Shakespeare buys house in Blackfriars area
Galileo says Copernicus was right; Vatican arrests him in 1616

1615

Miguel de Cervantes completes *Don Quixote* in Spain

1616

Daughter Judith marries Thomas Quiney
Shakespeare dies

1619

René Descartes establishes modern mathematics (analytic geometry)

1620

Pilgrims establish colony in North America at Plymouth Rock
Francis Bacon publishes *Novum Organum*, insisting that observation and experience are the basis of knowledge

1623

Anne Hathaway Shakespeare dies
Actors Condell and Heminge publish Shakespeare's collected plays in a single volume known as the First Folio

WORKS BY WILLIAM SHAKESPEARE

Editor's note: Many of the dates on this list are approximate. Since manuscripts identified with the date of writing do not exist, scholars have settled on the most accurate dates, either of the writing or of the first production of each play.

1 Henry VI (1591)

2 and *3 Henry VI* (1591–1592)

The Comedy of Errors; *Richard III*; Sonnets (1592–1593)

Titus Andronicus; *The Taming of the Shrew*; *The Two Gentlemen of Verona*; *Love's Labour's Lost*; *Venus and Adonis* published (1593)

The Rape of Lucrece published (1594)

A Midsummer Night's Dream; *Romeo and Juliet*; *Richard II* (1594–1595)

The Merchant of Venice (1595–1596)

King John (1596)

1 Henry IV (1597)

2 Henry IV; *Much Ado About Nothing* (1598)

Henry V; *As You Like It*; *Julius Caesar*; *The Merry Wives of Windsor*; "The Passionate Pilgrim" published (1599)

Twelfth Night; *Hamlet*; *Troilus and Cressida* (1600–1601)

"The Phoenix and the Turtle" (1601)

Othello (1602)

All's Well That Ends Well (1603)

Measure for Measure (1604)

King Lear; *Macbeth* (1606)

Antony and Cleopatra; *Coriolanus*; *Timon of Athens* (unfinished); *Pericles* completed (1607–1609)

Sonnets and "A Lover's Complaint" first published by Thomas Thorpe (1609)

Cymbeline (1610)

The Winter's Tale (1610–1611)

The Tempest (1611)

Henry VIII (1612–1613)

FOR FURTHER RESEARCH

ABOUT WILLIAM SHAKESPEARE AND HIS COMEDIES

Peter Alexander, *Shakespeare's Life and Art*. London: James Nisbet, 1939.

M.C. Bradbrook, *Shakespeare the Craftsman: The Clark Lectures, 1968*. London: Cambridge University Press, 1969.

Ivor Brown, *How Shakespeare Spent the Day*. New York: Hill and Wang, 1963.

S.T. Coleridge, *Shakespearean Criticism* (1811–1834), ed. T.M. Raysor. Cambridge, MA: Harvard University Press, 1930.

Hardin Craig and David Berington, *An Introduction to Shakespeare*. Rev ed. Glenview, IL: Scott, Foresman, 1975.

Edward Dowden, *Shakespeare: A Critical Study of His Mind and Art*. New York: Harper & Brothers, 1880.

Bernard Evans, *Shakespeare's Comedies*. London: Oxford University Press, 1960.

R.A. Foakes, *Shakespeare: The Dark Comedies to the Last Plays: from Satire to Celebration*. Charlottesville: University Press of Virginia, 1971.

Harley Granville-Barker and G.B. Harrison, eds., *A Companion to Shakespeare Studies*. New York: Cambridge University Press, 1934.

Alice Griffin, ed., *The Sources of Ten Shakespearean Plays*. New York: Thomas Y. Crowell, 1966.

G.K. Hunter, *William Shakespeare: The Later Comedies*. Harlow, Essex: Longmans, Green, 1962.

Dennis Kay, *Shakespeare: His Life, Work, and Era*. New York: William Morrow, 1992.

Jessica Kerr, *Shakespeare's Flowers*. Illustrated by Anne Ophelia Dowden. New York: Thomas Y. Crowell, 1969.

Victor Kiernan, *Shakespeare: Poet and Citizen.* New York: Verso, 1993.

Sidney Lee, *A Life of William Shakespeare.* New York: Dover, 1968.

John Middleton Murry, *Shakespeare.* New York: Harcourt, Brace, 1936.

Thomas Allen Nelson, *Shakespeare's Comic Theory: A Study of Art and Artifice in the Last Plays.* The Hague: Mouton, 1972.

A.L. Rowse, *Shakespeare the Man.* New York: Harper & Row, 1973.

S. Schoenbaum, *William Shakespeare: A Documentary Life.* New York: Oxford University Press in association with Scolar Press, 1975.

Edith Sitwell, *A Notebook on William Shakespeare.* Boston: Beacon Press, 1948.

Logan Pearsall Smith, *On Reading Shakespeare.* New York: Harcourt, Brace, 1933.

Theodore Spencer, *Shakespeare and the Nature of Man: Lowell Lectures, 1942.* 2nd ed. London: Collier-Macmillan, 1949.

Caroline F.E. Spurgeon, *Shakespeare's Imagery and What It Tells Us.* First copyright 1935. Reprint, New York: Cambridge University Press, 1987.

Derek Traversi, *William Shakespeare: The Early Comedies.* Harlow, Essex: Longmans, Green, 1960.

ABOUT ELIZABETHAN THEATERS AND TIMES

Joseph Quincy Adams, *Shakespearean Playhouses.* New York: Houghton Mifflin, 1917.

Maurice Ashley, *Great Britain to 1688.* Ann Arbor: University of Michigan Press, 1961.

Arthur Bryant, *Spirit of England.* London: William Collins, 1982.

Elizabeth Burton, *The Pageant of Elizabethan England.* New York: Charles Scribner's Sons, 1958.

John Cannon and Ralph Griffiths, *The Oxford Illustrated History of the British Monarchy.* New York: Oxford University Press, 1988.

Will and Ariel Durant, *The Age of Reason Begins: A History of European Civilization in the Period of Shakespeare, Bacon, Montaigne, Rembrandt, Galileo, and Descartes, 1558–1658.* Vol. 7 of *The Story of Civilization.* New York: Simon and Schuster, 1961.

Alfred Harbage, *Shakespeare's Audience.* New York: Columbia University Press, 1941.

G.B. Harrison, *Elizabethan Plays and Players.* Ann Arbor: University of Michigan Press, 1956.

A.V. Judges, *The Elizabethan Underworld.* New York: Octagon Books, 1965.

Walter Raleigh, ed., *Shakespeare's England.* 2 vols. Oxford: Clarendon Press, 1916.

Shakespeare and the Theatre. London: Members of the Shakespeare Association of London, 1927. (This is a series of papers by a variety of critics.)

E.M.W. Tillyard, *The Elizabethan World Picture.* New York: Macmillan, 1943.)

George Macaulay Trevelyan, *The Age of Shakespeare and the Stuart Period.* Vol. 2 of *Illustrated English Social History.* London: Longmans, Green, 1950.

INDEX